D1095115

Careers in Focus

OCEANOGRAPHY

Ferguson

An imprint of Infobase Publishing

Careers in Focus: Oceanography

Ferguson
An imprint of Infobase Publishing
132 West 31st Street
New York NY 10001

Library of Congress Cataloging-in-Publication Data

Careers in focus : oceanography.
    p. cm.
  Includes bibliographical references and index.
  ISBN-13: 978-0-8160-8026-7 (hardcover : alk. paper)
  ISBN-10: 0-8160-8026-7 (hardcover : alk. paper) 1. Oceanography—
Vocational guidance. 2. Marine sciences—Vocational guidance. I. Ferguson
Publishing.
  GC30.5.C37 2010
  551.46023—dc22

Ferguson books are available at special discounts when purchased in bulk quanti- ties for businesses, associations, institutions, or sales promotions. Please call our Special Sales Department in New York at (212) 967-8800 or (800) 322-8755.

You can find Ferguson on the World Wide Web at
http://www.infobasepublishing.com

Text design by David Strelecky
Composition by Mary Susan Ryan-Flynn
Cover printed by Art Print Company, Taylor, PA
Book printed and bound by Maple Press, York, PA
Date printed: December 2010
Printed in the United States of America

10 9 8 7 6 5 4 3 2 1

This book is printed on acid-free paper.

Table of Contents

Introduction 1

Aquarists 5

Atmospheric Scientists 12

Biological Oceanographers 22

Chemical Oceanographers 34

College Professors, Oceanography/
    Marine Science 42

Divers and Diving Technicians 59

Geological Oceanographers 73

Laboratory Testing Technicians 85

Marine Biologists 91

Marine Geophysicists 101

Marine Mammal Trainers 109

Marine Policy Experts and Lawyers 117

Marine Service Technicians 127

Marine Veterinarians 135

Ocean Engineers 144

Physical Oceanographers 153

Science Writers and Editors 162

Zoo and Aquarium Curators 176

Zoologists 185

Index 195

Introduction

Humans have landed on the moon; sent spacecraft to explore the red, rocky surface of Mars; and launched space telescopes that have photographed galaxies that are millions of miles away, but we have yet to completely explore Earth's oceans. This might be surprising to some, but our oceans are vast, deep expanses. In fact, oceans make up 72 percent of the surface of our planet (or 140 million square miles), and the average depth of the ocean is 12,200 feet. Additionally, the oceans are teeming with life. It is estimated that 80 percent of all life on Earth lives in the ocean, and scientists believe that there are at least 100 million unnamed species living on the floor of the ocean.

Many consider ocean exploration and research the last great frontier on Earth. With each passing day, oceanographers and other marine scientists learn more about the important role the ocean plays in our global ecosystem and how environmental degradation and pollution are hurting our great blue expanses and the organisms that live in them. But it's not all bad news. They are also making exciting discoveries—such as new plants and animals and medicinal and energy resources. For example, in 2008, oceanographers used a remotely operated submersible to explore the bottom of the Tasman Fracture, a deep ocean trench off the coast of Tasmania. At 11,483 feet down, they discovered new purple-spotted sea anemones. At 13,123 feet, according to PopSci.com, they spotted "a single never-before-seen carnivorous sea squirt with a funnel-shaped body that snapped shut like a Venus flytrap around any shrimp unfortunate enough to brush against it!" Discoveries like these, and the need to study and solve problems such as global warming, overfishing, and pollution, make it an exciting time to be an oceanographer.

Oceanography is a highly interdisciplinary science that covers all aspects of ocean study and exploration. It draws on the sciences of chemistry, biology, geology, botany, zoology, meteorology, physics, fluid mechanics, and applied mathematics. There are four main oceanography specialties: *biological, chemical, geological,* and *physical.* Biological oceanography is the study of the forms of life in the sea. Chemical oceanography is the study of the distribution of chemical compounds and chemical interactions that occur in the ocean and the seafloor. Geological oceanography is the study of the shape and material of the ocean floor. Physical oceanography is the study of water masses and ocean currents, the interaction between the ocean and atmosphere, and the relationship between the sea, weather, and climate.

There are opportunities for oceanographers and other marine scientists in state and federal agencies (such as the National Science Foundation; National Oceanic and Atmospheric Administration; Departments of Commerce, Defense, Energy, and Interior; National Aeronautics and Space Administration; Environmental Protection Agency; Biological Resources Discipline of the U.S. Geological Survey; Naval Oceanographic Office; Naval Research Laboratory; and Office of Naval Research), nonprofit organizations, colleges and universities, and in private industry (petroleum and gas exploration companies, renewable energy companies, pharmaceutical firms, and even for insurance companies that are trying to predict the effects of global warming).

Employment for all geoscientists (including oceanographers) will grow faster than the average for all occupations through 2018, according to the U.S. Department of Labor. Competitions for jobs in academia will be strong, but there are many other employment paths for aspiring marine science professionals.

The growth of technology will continue to create and expand job opportunities for those interested in the marine sciences. In general, oceanographers who also have training in other sciences or in engineering will probably have better opportunities for employment than those with training limited to oceanography.

The Oceanography Society says the growing interest in understanding and protecting the environment will also create new jobs. Careers related to fisheries resources, including basic research in biology and chemistry, as well as mariculture and sea ranching, will also increase. Because the oceans hold vast resources of commercially valuable minerals, employment opportunities will come from pharmaceutical and biotechnology companies and others interested in mining these substances for potential "miracle drugs" and other commercial uses. Continued deep-sea exploration made possible by underwater robotics and autonomous seacraft may also create more market opportunities for underwater research, with perhaps more international than U.S.-based employment potential.

In addition to oil and gas exploration, which can be harmful to ocean environments, scientists are also studying the ocean as a renewable energy resource. Advanced water power—such as ocean, river, and tidal currents and waves—may eventually become a significant source of renewable energy. And algae is being researched as a potential biofuel. These developments provide another great opportunity for marine scientists.

Each article in *Careers in Focus: Oceanography* discusses a particular occupation in detail. Some of the articles appear in Ferguson's *Encyclopedia of Careers and Vocational Guidance; others have been written especially for this book.* Since the last edition of this book, each article has been updated and revised with the latest information from the U.S. Department of Labor and other sources. Each article is broken down in the following manner.

The **Quick Facts** section provides a brief summary of the career, including recommended school subjects, personal skills, work environment, minimum educational requirements, salary ranges, certification or licensing requirements, and employment outlook. This section also provides acronyms and identification numbers for the following government classification indexes: the *Dictionary of Occupational Titles* (DOT), the *Guide for Occupational Exploration* (GOE), the National Occupational Classification (NOC) Index, and the Occupational Information Network (O*NET)-Standard Occupational Classification System (SOC) index. The DOT, GOE, and O*NET-SOC indexes have been created by the U.S. government; the NOC index is Canada's career classification system. Readers can use the identification numbers listed in the Quick Facts section to access further information about a career. Print editions of the DOT (*Dictionary of Occupational Titles.* Indianapolis, Ind.: JIST Works, 1991) and GOE (*Guide for Occupational Exploration.* Indianapolis, Ind.: JIST Works, 2001) are available at libraries. Electronic versions of the DOT (http://www.oalj.dol.gov/libdot.htm), NOC (http://www5.hrsdc.gc.ca/NOC), and O*NET-SOC (http://online.onetcenter.org) are available on the Internet. When no DOT, GOE, NOC, or O*NET-SOC numbers are listed, this means that the U.S. Department of Labor or Human Resources and Skills Development Canada have not created a numerical designation for this career. In this instance, you will see the acronym "N/A," or not available.

The **Overview** section is a brief introductory description of the duties and responsibilities involved in this career. Oftentimes, a career may have a variety of job titles. When this is the case, alternative career titles are presented. Employment statistics are also provided, when available. The **History** section describes the history of the particular job as it relates to the overall development of its industry or field. **The Job** describes the primary and secondary duties of the job. **Requirements** discusses high school and postsecondary education and training requirements, any certification or licensing that is necessary, and other personal requirements for success in the job. **Exploring** offers suggestions on how to gain experience in or knowledge of the particular job before making a firm educational and financial commitment. The focus is on what can be done while still in high school (or in the early years of college) to gain a better understanding of the job. The **Employers** section gives an overview of typical places of employment for the job. **Starting Out** discusses the best ways to land that first job, be it through the college career services office, newspaper ads, Internet employment sites, or personal contact. The **Advancement** section describes what kind of career path to expect from the job and how to get there. **Earnings** lists salary ranges and describes the typical fringe benefits. The **Work Environment** section describes the typical surroundings and conditions of employment—whether indoors or outdoors, noisy or quiet, social or independent. Also discussed are typical hours worked, any seasonal fluctuations, and the stresses and strains of the job. The **Outlook** section summarizes the job in terms of the general economy and industry projections. For the most part, Outlook information is obtained from the U.S. Bureau of Labor Statistics and is supplemented by information gathered from professional associations. Job growth terms follow those used in the *Occupational Outlook Handbook*. Growth described as "much faster than the average" means an increase of 20 percent or more. Growth described as "faster than the average" means an increase of 14 to 19 percent. Growth described as "about as fast as the average" means an increase of 7 to 13 percent. Growth described as "more slowly than the average" means an increase of 3 to 6 percent. "Little or no change" means a decrease of 2 percent to an increase of 2 percent. "Decline" means a decrease of 3 percent or more. Each article ends with **For More Information,** which lists organizations that provide information on training, education, internships, scholarships, and job placement.

Careers in Focus: Oceanography also includes photos, informative sidebars, and interviews with professionals in the field.

Aquarists

OVERVIEW

Aquarists (pronounced, like "aquarium," with the accent on the second syllable) work for aquariums, oceanariums, and marine research institutes. They maintain aquatic exhibits. Among other duties, they feed the fish, check water quality, clean the tanks, and collect and transport new specimens.

HISTORY

In 1853, the world's first public aquarium opened in Regents Park in London. Similar public aquariums opened throughout England, France, and Germany over the next 15 years. Many of the early aquariums closed because the fish could not survive in the conditions provided. By the early 1870s, knowledge of aeration, filtering, and water temperature had increased, and new aquariums opened.

In 1856, the U.S. government established what is today the Division of Fishes of the Smithsonian Institution's National Museum of Natural History. Over the next 50 years interest in fish and their environments grew rapidly. The Scripps Institution of Oceanography was established in 1903, and the Woods Hole Oceanographic Institute was established in 1930.

Today's notable aquariums include the John G. Shedd Aquarium, Chicago; the National Aquarium, Baltimore; the Georgia Aquarium, Atlanta, Georgia; the New York Aquarium, New York City; the Steinhart Aquarium, San Francisco; and the Audubon Aquarium of the Americas, New Orleans. Many aquariums re-create diverse aquatic environments, such as coral reefs, river bottoms, or various coastlines, in large tanks.

Aquariums on the Web

Here are some of the most well-known aquariums and oceanariums in the United States. Visit their Web sites to learn about their operating hours and programs that are available for young people.

Audubon Aquarium of the Americas (New Orleans)
http://www.auduboninstitute.org/aquarium.html

Georgia Aquarium (Atlanta)
http://www.georgiaaquarium.org

John G. Shedd Aquarium (Chicago)
http://www.sheddaquarium.org

Miami Seaquarium (Miami, Fla.)
http://www.miamiseaquarium.com

Monterey Bay Aquarium (Monterey, Calif.)
http://www.montereybayaquarium.org

Mystic Aquarium and Institute for Exploration (Mystic, Conn.)
http://www.mysticaquarium.org

National Aquarium Baltimore
http://www.aqua.org

New England Aquarium (Boston)
http://www.neaq.org

New York Aquarium (New York City)
http://www.nyaquarium.com

Oregon Coast Aquarium (Newport)
http://www.aquarium.org

Seattle Aquarium
http://www.seattleaquarium.org

Steinhart Aquarium (San Francisco)
http://www.calacademy.org/academy/exhibits/aquarium

Waikiki Aquarium (Waikiki, Hawaii)
http://www.waquarium.org

Some aquariums also have oceanariums—huge tanks that allow visitors to view marine animals from above as well as from the sides. Popular oceanariums include those at the Miami Seaquarium in Miami, Florida, and the Monterey Bay Aquarium in Monterey, California.

THE JOB

Aquarists work for aquariums, oceanariums, and marine research institutes. Aquarists are not animal trainers and do not work on marine shows. They do, however, support the staff who do. Their work is generally technical and requires a strong science background. With increased experience and education, aquarists may, in time, become involved in research efforts at their institution or become promoted to higher professional positions such as curator.

Aquarists' job duties are similar to those of zookeepers. Aquarists feed fish and other marine animals, maintain exhibits, and conduct research. They work on breeding, conservation, and educational programs.

Aquarists clean and take care of tanks every day. They make sure pumps are working, check water temperatures, clean glass, and sift sand. Some exhibits have to be scrubbed by hand. Aquarists also change the water and vacuum tanks routinely. They water plants in marsh or pond exhibits.

Food preparation and feeding are important tasks for aquarists. Some animals eat live food and others eat cut-up food mixtures. Some animals need special diets prepared and may have to be individually fed.

Aquarists carefully observe all the animals in their care. They must understand their normal habits (including mating, feeding, sleeping, and moving) in order to be able to judge when something is wrong. Aquarists write daily reports and keep detailed records of animal behavior.

Many aquarists are in charge of collecting and stocking plants and animals for exhibits. They may have to make several trips a year to gather live specimens.

REQUIREMENTS

High School

If you want to become an aquarist, get your start in high school. Take as many science classes as possible; biology and zoology are especially important. Learn to pay attention to detail; marine science involves a good deal of careful record keeping.

An aquarist (*left*) and his assistant lift a live zebra shark out of the water for examination at the PPG Aquarium in Pittsburgh, Pennsylvania. (*Steve Adams, AP Photo*/The Tribune-Review)

Postsecondary Training
Most aquariums, along with other institutions that hire aquarists, require that an applicant have a bachelor's degree in biological sciences, preferably with course work in such areas as parasitology (the study of parasites and their hosts), ichthyology (the study of fishes), or other aquatic sciences. As the care of captive animals becomes a more complex discipline, it's no longer enough to apply without a four-year degree.

Certification or Licensing
Aquarists must be able to dive, in both contained water to feed fish and maintain tanks, and in open water on trips to collect new specimens. You'll need to have scuba certification, with a rescue diver classification, for this job. Organizations such as PADI provide basic certification. Potential employers will expect you to be able to pass a diving physical examination before taking you on as an aquarist. You may also need to have a special collector's permit from the state in which you work that allows you to gather samples for your aquarium.

Other Requirements
As an aquarist, you may be required to travel at different times throughout the year, to participate in research expeditions and col-

lecting trips. On a more basic level, aquarists need to be in good physical shape, with good hearing and visual acuity. Some employers also require a certain strength level—say, the ability to regularly exert 100 pounds of force—since equipment, feed, and the animals themselves can be heavy and often unwieldy. Good communication and teamwork skills are also important.

EXPLORING

In addition to formal education, many aquariums, like other types of museums, look for a strong interest in the field before hiring an applicant. Most often, they look for a history of volunteering. That means you need to look for every avenue you can find to work around fish or other animals. Do as much as your schedule allows. Even working part time or volunteering at a local pet store counts. Also, be sure to ask your career guidance counselor for information on marine science careers and opportunities for summer internships or college scholarships offered by larger institutes.

You should also consider joining the Association of Zoos and Aquariums (AZA), which offers an associate membership category "for zoo and aquarium professionals, as well as other interested parties, who want to support and forward the mission, vision, and goals of AZA."

EMPLOYERS

Aquarists most often work in zoos, public aquariums, or in research jobs with marine science institutes.

STARTING OUT

Full-time jobs for aquarists can be scarce, especially for those just starting in the field. Part-time or volunteer positions with zoos, aquariums, science institutes, nature centers, or even pet stores could provide valuable preliminary experience that may eventually lead to a full-time position.

ADVANCEMENT

The usual career path for an aquarist progresses from intern/volunteer through part-time work to full-fledged aquarist, senior aquarist, supervisor, and finally, curator. Each step along the path requires additional experience and often additional education. Curators generally are expected to have a Ph.D. in a relevant marine science discipline, for example. The career path of an aquarist depends on how much hands-on work they like to do with animals. Other options are available for aquarists who are looking for a less "down and dirty" experience.

EARNINGS

Aquariums often are nonprofit institutions, limiting the earnings ability in this job somewhat. In general, aquarists make between $23,000 and $40,000 a year. Salaries for nonfarm animal caretakers (a career category that includes aquarists) ranged from less than $15,590 to $31,660 or more in 2009, according to the U.S. Department of Labor.

Aquariums offer fairly extensive benefits, including health insurance, 401(k) plans, continuing education opportunities, tuition reimbursement, and reciprocal benefits with many other cultural institutions.

WORK ENVIRONMENT

Aquarists may work indoors or outdoors, depending on the facility for which they work and the exhibit to which they're assigned. Aquarists spend a lot of time in the water. Their day will be filled with a variety of tasks, some repetitive, like feeding, others unusual, such as working with rescued marine mammals, perhaps. In the beginning, aquarists work under the supervision of a senior aquarist or supervisor and may work as part of a team. Aquarists also can expect to travel as part of the job.

OUTLOOK

Overall, employment opportunities for animal care and service workers are expected to grow much faster than the average of all occupations through 2018, according to the U.S. Department of Labor. However, there is, in general, little change in the availability of positions for aquarists. While terrestrial zoos have begun to add aquarium complexes to their campuses in growing numbers, an actual boom in the construction of new aquariums is unlikely at this time. Many aquarists do advance to other positions, however, so openings do become available. Aquarists with advanced degrees and training who are willing to relocate will have the best employment opportunities.

FOR MORE INFORMATION

Visit the alliance's Web site for information on marine mammals, internships, and publications.

Alliance of Marine Mammal Parks and Aquariums
E-mail: ammpa@aol.com
http://www.ammpa.org

For information on membership, a list of accredited zoos throughout the world, and careers in aquatic and marine science, including job listings, contact

Association of Zoos and Aquariums
8403 Colesville Road, Suite 710
Silver Spring, MD 20910-3314
Tel: 301-562-0777
http://www.aza.org

For information on diving instruction and certification, contact

Professional Association of Diving Instructors (PADI)
30151 Tomas Street
Rancho Santa Margarita, CA 92688-2125
Tel: 800-729-7234
http://www.padi.com

Atmospheric Scientists

QUICK FACTS

School Subjects
Earth science
Geography
Physics

Personal Skills
Helping/teaching
Technical/scientific

Work Environment
Indoors and outdoors
One location with some
travel

Minimum Education Level
Bachelor's degree

Salary Range
$40,560 to $84,710 to
$127,250+

Certification or Licensing
Recommended

Outlook
Faster than the average

DOT
025

GOE
02.01.01

NOC
2114

O*NET-SOC
19-2021.00

OVERVIEW

Atmospheric science is often defined as the study of the atmosphere through a combination of meteorology and other physical sciences. *Atmospheric scientists,* also known as *meteorologists,* study weather conditions and forecast weather changes. By using numerical forecasting models and analyzing weather maps covering large geographic areas and related charts, like upper-air maps and soundings, they can predict the movement of fronts, precipitation, and pressure areas. They forecast such data as temperature, winds, precipitation, cloud cover, and flying and boating conditions. Atmospheric scientists conduct research on such subjects as atmospheric electricity, clouds, precipitation, hurricanes, and data collected from weather satellites to predict future weather patterns and develop increased accuracy in weather study and forecasting. Other areas of research used to forecast weather may include ocean currents and temperature. Atmospheric scientists who focus on marine weather study how the ocean affects atmospheric conditions and how weather affects ocean life. The American Meteorological Society has more than 14,000 members.

HISTORY

Mariners have sought to understand and predict the weather ever since the first ships were built by the ancient Egyptians in 4000 B.C. Bad weather could delay or even cancel a voyage, and over the years many ships were lost as a result of unpredictable weather conditions. The philosopher Aristotle is considered to be the father of meteorology. Around 340 B.C., he wrote *Meteorologica*, which was the first study of the atmosphere.

The basic meteorological instruments were invented hundreds of years ago. Galileo invented the thermometer in 1593 and Evangelista Torricelli invented the barometer in 1643. Devices that measured humidity, wind speed, and other atmospheric conditions were also invented. During the following centuries, scientists from around the world studied atmospheric conditions on land and sea and began to see the links between atmospheric conditions and the ocean. Unfortunately, scientists from different countries found it hard to share research since no standardized marine meteorological measurements existed. From August-September 1853, the first international meteorological conference was held in Brussels, Belgium. According to the World Meteorological Organization (WMO), the conference was held for the purpose of "establishing a uniform system of meteorological observations at sea, and of concurring in a general plan of observation on the winds and currents of the ocean." The first International Meteorological Congress was held in Vienna, Austria, in 1873. The Congress is credited with being the impetus for the founding of the International Meteorological Association, the predecessor organization to the WMO (an agency of the United Nations and a leader in the study of atmospheric science today).

Observations of the upper atmosphere from balloons and airplanes started after World War I. Not until World War II, however, was great financial support given to the development of meteorology. Accurate forecasting of weather conditions played a key role in the success of air, sea, and land battles.

In 1970, the U.S. government created the National Oceanic and Atmospheric Administration to study the interactions between weather and the world's oceans.

More accurate instruments for measuring and observing weather conditions, new systems of communication, and the development of satellites, radar, and supercomputers to process and analyze weather data have helped atmospheric scientists and the general public to get a better understanding of the atmosphere and how it interacts with the land and oceans.

THE JOB

Meteorology is an observational science: the study of the atmosphere, weather, and climate. Although most people think of weather forecasting when they think of meteorology, atmospheric scientists do many other kinds of work also. They research subjects ranging from radioactive fallout to the dynamics of hurricanes. They study the ozone levels in the stratosphere. Some teach in colleges and universities. A few meteorologists work in radio and televised weather forecasting.

Meteorologists generally specialize in one branch of this rapidly developing science; however, the lines of specialization are not clearly drawn and meteorologists often work in more than one area of specialization. The largest group of specialists are called *operational meteorologists*, the technical name for weather forecasters, who collect and interpret current weather and ocean data, such as air pressure, temperature, humidity, and wind velocity, reported by observers, weather satellites, weather radar, and remote sensors in many parts of the world. They use this data to make short- and long-range forecasts for given regions. Operational meteorologists also use Doppler radar, which detects rotational patterns in violent thunderstorms, in order to better predict tornadoes, thunderstorms, and flash floods, as well as their direction and intensity.

Climatologists study past records to discover weather patterns for a given region. The climatologist compiles, makes statistical analyses of, and interprets data on temperature, sunlight, rainfall, humidity, and wind for a particular area over a long period of time for use in scientific research, weather forecasting, aviation, agriculture, commerce, and public health.

Applied meteorologists use meteorological research for practical applications. For example, they help ferry operators, oil and gas exploration companies, and cruise lines avoid dangerous weather conditions such as hurricanes.

Dynamic meteorologists study the physical laws related to air currents. *Physical meteorologists* study the physical nature of the atmosphere including its chemical composition and electrical, acoustical, and optical properties. *Environmental meteorologists* study air pollution, global warming, ozone depletion, water shortages, and other environmental problems and write impact statements about their findings. *Industrial meteorologists* work in a variety of private industries, focusing their expertise on such problems as smoke control and air pollution. *Synoptic meteorologists* study large-scale patterns responsible for our daily weather as well as find new ways to forecast weather events by using mathematical models and computers. *Flight meteorologists* fly in aircraft to study hurricanes and other weather phenomena.

One new major area of study for atmospheric scientists is *global change research*, also known as *earth systems science*. Nearly all of the world's major scientists agree that the earth's climate is undergoing major changes as a result of global warming. These changes will affect billions of people. Meteorologists are trying to understand the role that clouds, snow, and other atmospheric phenomena play in fueling or reducing global climate change. According to the American Meteorological Society, they are also "studying interactions among the atmosphere and oceans, the polar ice caps, and the earth's plants and animals" to better understand short- and long-term climate changes.

The tools used by meteorologists include weather balloons, instrumented aircraft, radar, satellites, and computers. Instrumented aircraft are high-performance airplanes designed to sample and observe many kinds of weather. Radar is used to detect a variety of precipitation types, and the motions within clouds that may lead to violent weather. Doppler radar can measure wind speed and direction. It has become the best tool for the short-term prediction of severe weather. Satellites use advanced remote sensing to measure temperature, wind, and other characteristics of the atmosphere at many levels. The entire surface of the earth can be observed with satellites.

The introduction of computers has changed research and forecasting of weather. The fastest computers are used in atmospheric research on major issues such as global warming/climate change, as well as large-scale weather forecasting.

Atmospheric scientists who specialize in marine meteorology work closely with other marine science professionals—especially physical oceanographers, but also other types of oceanographers, hydrologists, mathematicians, and computer scientists.

REQUIREMENTS

High School
You can best prepare for a college major in the atmospheric sciences by taking high school courses in mathematics, geography, computer science, physics, and chemistry. A good command of English is essential because you must be able to describe complex weather events and patterns in a clear and concise way. If you plan to specialize in marine meteorology, take earth science and other classes that will help you learn about oceans and the environment.

Postsecondary Training
Although some beginners in meteorological work have majored in subjects related to meteorology, the usual minimal requirement for work in this field is a bachelor's degree in meteorology. For entry-level positions in the federal government, you must have a bachelor's

Max Mayfield, who served as the director of the National Hurricane Center from 2000 to 2007, points to the eye of Hurricane Rita as he announces that its center has officially reached land along the Texas–Louisiana Gulf Coast border. *(Andy Newman, AP Photo)*

degree (not necessarily in meteorology) with at least 24 semester hours of meteorology courses, including six hours in the analysis and prediction of weather systems, two hours of remote sensing of the atmosphere or instrumentation, and three hours of physical meteorology. Other required courses include ordinary differential equations, calculus, physics, physical hydrology, radiative transfer, aeronomy (the study of the upper atmosphere), statistics, computer science, advanced thermodynamics, advanced electricity and magnetism, chemistry, physical oceanography, physical climatology, light and optics, and computer science. Advanced graduate training in meteorology and related areas is required for research and teaching positions, as well as for other high-level positions in meteorology. Doctorates are quite common among high-level personnel.

Because the armed forces require the services of so many meteorologists, they have programs to send recently commissioned, new college graduates to civilian universities for intensive work in meteorology.

Certification or Licensing
The American Meteorological Society provides the following certification designations: certified broadcast meteorologist and certified

consulting meteorologist. The National Weather Association offers the Weathercaster Seal of Approval. Contact these organizations for information on certification requirements.

Other Requirements
To be a successful atmospheric scientist, you must be attentive to detail, highly organized, and able to communicate complex theories and events, orally and in writing. Meteorologists who work in broadcasting must have especially good communication skills in order to convey forecasts and scientific information to their audiences.

EXPLORING
There are several ways that you can explore career possibilities in meteorology. Each year, for example, the federal government's National Weather Service accepts a limited number of student volunteers, mostly college students but also a few high school students. Some universities offer credit for a college student's volunteer work in connection with meteorology courses. The National Oceanographic and Atmospheric Administration has details about the volunteer program. The armed forces can also be a means of gaining experience in meteorology.

Arrange for an information interview with a meteorologist who works at a local airport, marine meteorology research institution, or college offering classes in meteorology. Your high school counselor should be able to help you set up this meeting. You can also get additional information from organizations, such as those listed at the end of this article.

The American Meteorological Society offers a comprehensive career guide on its Web site, http://www.ametsoc.org/atmoscareers. Content includes suggestions on the types of course work and training to consider during the college years, various career opportunities, typical employers and workplaces, job and salary outlook statistics, and certification information.

You can also read books about meteorology. Here are two suggestions: *Meteorology Today: An Introduction to Weather, Climate, and the Environment,* 9th ed., by Donald C. Ahrens, and *The Atmosphere: An Introduction to Meteorology,* 11th ed., by Frederick K. Lutgens. Ask your school or community library to provide more suggestions.

EMPLOYERS
The American Meteorological Society has more than 14,000 members. The largest employer of meteorologists is the federal government.

Most of its civilian meteorologists work for the National Oceanic and Atmospheric Administration's (NOAA's) National Weather Service forecast offices across the country. The NOAA operates a dozen environmental research laboratories, including the Atlantic Oceanographic and Meteorological Laboratory (which houses the Hurricane Research Division) and the Climate Analysis Branch of the Earth System Research Laboratory. Atmospheric scientists are also employed by the National Center for Atmospheric Research, which is sponsored by the National Science Foundation. The remainder of the meteorologists worked mainly in research and development or management. Additionally, several hundred civilian meteorologists work at the Department of Defense. Many opportunities are also available in the armed forces (such as in the Office of Naval Research Marine Meteorology Program) and in educational settings. There are hundreds of meteorologists teaching at institutions of higher education.

Other meteorologists work for private weather consulting firms, engineering service firms, commercial airlines, radio and television stations, computer and data processing services, and companies that design and manufacture meteorological instruments and aircraft and missiles.

STARTING OUT

You can enter the field of atmospheric science in a number of ways. For example, new graduates may find positions through career services offices at the colleges and universities where they have studied. National Weather Service volunteers may receive permanent positions as meteorologists upon completing their formal training. Members of the armed forces who have done work in meteorology often assume positions in meteorology when they return to civilian life. In fact, the armed forces give preference in the employment of civilian meteorologists to former military personnel with appropriate experience. Individuals interested in teaching and research careers generally assume these positions upon receiving their doctorates in meteorology or related subjects.

Other federal employers of meteorologists include the National Science Foundation, Department of Defense, the National Aeronautics and Space Administration, and the Department of Agriculture.

ADVANCEMENT

Atmospheric scientists employed by the National Weather Service and other federal government agencies advance according to civil service regulations. After meeting certain experience and education requirements, they advance to classifications that carry more pay and, often, more responsibility. Opportunities available to meteorologists employed by airlines are more limited. A few of these workers, however, do advance to such positions as flight dispatcher and to administrative and supervisory positions. A few meteorologists go into business for themselves by establishing their own weather consulting services. Atmospheric scientists who are employed in teaching and research in colleges and universities advance through academic promotions or by assuming administrative positions in the university setting.

EARNINGS

The U.S. Department of Labor reports that median annual earnings of atmospheric scientists were $84,710 in 2009. Salaries ranged from less than $40,560 to more than $127,250. The average salary for meteorologists employed by the federal government was $94,210 in 2009.

Meteorologists with a bachelor of science degree are usually hired by the National Weather Service at the GS-5 to GS-7 grade levels; base salaries at these levels ranged from $27,431 (GS-5) to $30,577 (GS-6) to $33,979 (GS-7) in 2010. Those with a master of science degree enter at the GS-7 to GS-9 levels, which had base pay that ranged from $33,979 (GS-7) to $37,631 (GS-8) to $41,563 (GS-9). Meteorologists with Ph.D.'s enter at the GS-9 to GS-11 levels, which ranged from $41,563 (GS-9) to $45,771 (GS-10) to $50,287 (GS-11).

In broadcast meteorology, salaries vary greatly. Television weathercasters earn salaries that range from $16,000 to $1,000,000 or more.

Benefits for atmospheric scientists depend on the employer; however, they usually include such items as health insurance, retirement or 401(k) plans, and paid vacation days. Self-employed atmospheric scientists must provide their own benefits.

WORK ENVIRONMENT

Weather stations operate 24 hours a day, seven days a week. This means that some atmospheric scientists, often on a rotating basis, work evenings and weekends. Although most of these weather stations are at airports located near cities, a number of weather stations are located in isolated and remote areas. One of the most remote meteorological posts is in the Antarctic. However, it provides some of the most interesting and relevant data in meteorology. In these places, the life of an atmospheric scientist can be quiet and lonely. Operational meteorologists often work overtime during weather emergencies such as hurricanes. Meteorologists who work in college and university settings enjoy the same working conditions as other professors.

OUTLOOK

According to the *Occupational Outlook Handbook*, employment for meteorologists should grow faster than the average for all careers through 2018. Despite this prediction, there will be strong competition for jobs.

Opportunities for atmospheric scientists in private industry are expected to be better than in the federal government. Private weather consulting firms are able to provide more detailed information than the National Weather Service to weather-sensitive industries, such as farmers, oil and gas exploration companies, commodity investors, radio and television stations, and utilities, transportation, and construction firms.

Employment should be fair for broadcast meteorologists. This field is highly competitive, and the best opportunities will be available to those with certification and strong broadcasting skills.

Overall, opportunities will be best for those with advanced degrees and certification.

FOR MORE INFORMATION

For information on careers, certification, a searchable database of postsecondary training programs in meteorology, answers to frequently asked questions about meteorology, and scholarships, contact

American Meteorological Society
45 Beacon Street
Boston, MA 02108-3693
Tel: 617-227-2425
E-mail: amsinfo@ametsoc.org
http://www.ametsoc.org

For information on industrial and applied meteorology, contact
National Council of Industrial Meteorologists
PO Box 721165
Norman, OK 73070-4892
Tel: 405-329-8707
E-mail: info@ncim.org
http://www.ncim.org

This government agency is concerned with describing and predicting changes in the environment, as well as managing marine and coastal resources.

National Oceanographic and Atmospheric Administration
1401 Constitution Avenue, NW, Room 5128
Washington, DC 20230-0001
http://www.careers.noaa.gov
http://www.noaa.gov

Visit the association's Web site for a list of schools with degree programs in meteorology or atmospheric science and information on scholarships and membership for college students.

National Weather Association
228 West Millbrook Road
Raleigh, NC 27609-4304
Tel: 919-845-1546
http://www.nwas.org

The NWS is an agency of the National Oceanographic and Atmospheric Administration. Visit its Web site for comprehensive information on weather forecasting and weather phenomena.

National Weather Service (NWS)
1325 East-West Highway
Silver Spring, MD 20910-3280
http://www.nws.noaa.gov

This United Nations agency focuses on meteorology (weather and climate), operational hydrology, and related geophysical sciences.

World Meteorological Organization
http://www.wmo.int

Biological Oceanographers

QUICK FACTS

School Subjects
Biology
Chemistry
Earth science
Mathematics

Personal Skills
Communication/ideas
Technical/scientific

Work Environment
Indoors and outdoors
One location with some
   travel

Minimum Education Level
Bachelor's degree

Salary Range
$43,140 to $81,220 to
   $161,260+

Certification or Licensing
Voluntary

Outlook
Faster than the average

DOT
024

GOE
02.03.03

NOC
2113

O*NET-SOC
19-2042.00

OVERVIEW

Oceanographers study the earth's oceans through observations, surveys, and experiments. *Biological oceanographers* are specialized oceanographers who study marine organisms—from bacteria and viruses, to plants, to sea lions, fishes, and whales. They study their activities, distribution, and their relationship to one another and their environments.

HISTORY

People have studied the oceans of the world and the organisms that live in them for thousands of years. In fact, the Greek philosopher Aristotle wrote *Historia Animalium*, the first treatise on marine biology in 325 B.C.

Scientists, explorers, and mariners continued to study the oceans for the next 2,000 years, but it was not until the 1800s that the seeds of modern oceanography were planted as a result of ocean explorations by scientists from a variety of countries. Some noteworthy expeditions include those of Sir John Ross in the Arctic Ocean (1817–18), Charles Darwin (1831–36) to many regions in the Pacific Ocean, Sir James Ross (the nephew of Sir John Ross) to Antarctica (1839–43), Charles Wyville Thomson and John Murray to all the oceans of the world except the Arctic (1872–76), and Alexander Agassiz (1877–80) to areas of the South Pacific. Other significant developments that fueled the work of early biological oceanographers were the founding of the first U.S. marine station on Penikese

Books to Read: Ocean Life

Barr, Nevada. *Endangered Species*. Reprint ed. New York: Berkley Books, 2008.

Crist, Darlene Trew, Gail Scowcroft, James M. Harding Jr., and Sylvia Earle. *World Ocean Census:* A Global Survey of Marine Life. Richmond Hill, O.N. Canada: Firefly Books, 2009.

Dinwiddie, Robert, Louise Thomas, and Fabien Cousteau. *Ocean*. Reprint ed. New York: DK Publishing, 2008.

Gerdes, Louise I. *Endangered Oceans*. Farmington Hills, Mich.: Greenhaven Press, 2009.

Mackay, Richard. *The Atlas of Endangered Species*. Berkeley, Calif.: University of California Press, 2008.

McKay, George. (ed.) *The Encyclopedia of Animals: A Complete Visual Guide*. Berkeley, Calif.: University of California Press, 2004.

Perrin, William F., Bernd Würsig, and J.G.M Thewissen. (eds.) *Encyclopedia of Marine Mammals*. 2d ed. Maryland Heights, Mo.: Academic Press, 2008.

Island in Massachusetts in 1873; the construction of the USS *Albatross* (1884), which was used specifically to conduct scientific research at sea; the establishment of the Marine Biological Laboratory at Woods Hole, Massachusetts (1888); the establishment of the International Council for the Exploration of the Sea (1902), which studied ocean conditions that affected fisheries in the North Atlantic; and the establishment of the Scripps Institution of Biological Research (now known as the Scripps Institution of Oceanography) in 1903.

From 1925 to 1927, a German research expedition aboard the *Meteor* studied the physical oceanography of the Atlantic Ocean. This expedition marked the beginning of the modern age of oceanographic investigation, according to *Invitation to Oceanography*, by Paul R. Pinet.

Today, biological oceanographers continue to study the world's oceans. They are in strong demand to study and find solutions to global warming, pollution, overfishing, and declining species diversity.

THE JOB

Biological oceanographers study the many forms of life in the sea. Unlike *marine biologists*, who study the physiology and habits of individual organisms, biological oceanographers strive to understand the relationship between living organisms and their environment. They study patterns in population density, life cycles, physical and chemical factors that influence the distribution and volume of ocean life, and the cycling of nutrients (nitrogen, phosphorus, etc.) through the marine food chain. They also examine the distribution of plants and animals through the ocean, the relationships between different organisms, and the impact of human behavior on ocean life.

Biological oceanographers conduct research in the field. During field research they might travel on a research vessel and conduct research by lowering instruments and water sampling gear into the ocean from the ship or they may dive into the water to observe and gather samples of marine organisms such as zooplankton. They might travel deep beneath the ocean surface in an underwater submersible vehicle to study the biological communities that reside near deep-sea hydrothermal vents.

Oceanographers also spend a lot of time indoors in laboratories and offices analyzing data, samples, and specimens gathered during field research. Technology is also allowing biological oceanographers to conduct research without ever leaving their offices. Satellites, airborne sensors, programmable buoys, and other remote sensing devices are just a few of the technologies biological oceanographers use in their work. They also use mathematical modeling software that helps them answer questions that can not be completely answered by hands-on research, such as the effects that global warming or pollution will have on the oceans over a long period of time.

Like other oceanography specialties, biological oceanography is a highly interdisciplinary field. Biological oceanographers work closely with chemical, physical, and geological oceanographers, marine biologists, geophysicists, biochemists, biogeochemists, geologists, microbiologists, and molecular biologists.

Some biological oceanographers work at colleges and universities. Academic positions usually entail a combination of teaching and research. Experienced oceanographers who work for large universities may devote the lion's share of their time to research, teaching only one or two classes each year. Oceanographers who teach at smaller institutions or at the undergraduate level, on the other hand, may be entirely occupied with teaching. Within academia, the two largest employers of oceanographers are Woods Hole Oceanographic Institution and the Scripps Institution of Oceanography, though many coastal universities also maintain excellent oceanographic programs. Some oceanographers write books and articles about the field and their discoveries.

REQUIREMENTS

High School

You will need at least a bachelor's degree to work as an oceanographer. To prepare for your postsecondary education, take four years of college preparatory courses while in high school. Science courses, including geology, biology, and chemistry, and math classes, such as linear algebra, trigonometry, calculus, and statistics, are especially important to take. Take English and speech classes to hone your communication skills. Other important classes include computer science and foreign languages.

Postsecondary Training

A bachelor's degree is the minimum educational requirement to enter the field, but most employers require a master's degree in oceanography, biology, chemistry, marine science, or a related field. Many biological oceanographers earn bachelor's degrees in biology or a related major before continuing their education to earn a graduate degree in oceanography. A Ph.D. in oceanography is required for most positions in research and teaching. More than 100 institutions offer programs in marine studies, and more than 35 universities have graduate programs leading to a doctoral degree in oceanography.

Typical classes in a biological oceanography program include Introduction to Biological Oceanography, Marine Biology, Marine Microbiology, Marine Systems Ecology, Environmental Physiology of Marine Animals, Molecular Approach to Biological Oceanography, Marine Bioorganic Chemistry, and Coastal Pollution and Bioremediation.

Many oceanography students participate in internships or work as teaching assistants while in college to gain hands-on experience in the field. The American Society of Limnology and Oceanography offers a list of internships at its Web site, http://www.aslo.org.

Certification or Licensing

Oceanographers may scuba dive when conducting research. Organizations such as PADI provide basic certification (see For More Information for contact details).

Other Requirements

To be a successful oceanographer, you should have a keen interest in biological science, possess strong observational skills, be willing to work hard and at irregular hours, have intellectual curiosity, enjoy working outdoors, have excellent communication skills, and be able to work well with people from a variety of backgrounds. Oceanographers who conduct field research should be willing to work away from home for long periods of time. Prospective oceanographers should also be able to discriminate detail among objects in terms of their shape, size, color, or markings. Other important skills include perseverance, open-mindedness, and integrity.

EXPLORING

Read books and visit Web sites about general oceanography and the specialization of biological oceanography. Here is one book suggestion: *Biological Oceanography*, by Charles B. Miller. Your school or local librarian can suggest others. You can also visit the Sea Grant Marine Careers Web site (http://www.marinecareers.net) for information on careers, internships, volunteerships, and other activities, such as sea camps.

Obviously, if you live near coastal regions, you will have an easier time becoming familiar with oceans and ocean life than if you are land-bound. However, some institutions offer work or leisure-time experiences that provide participants with opportunities to explore particular aspects of oceanography. Possible opportunities include work in marine or conservation fisheries or onboard seagoing vessels or field experiences in studying rocks, minerals, or aquatic life. If you live or travel near one of the oceanography research centers, such as Woods Hole Oceanographic Institution on Cape Cod, the University of Miami's Rosenstiel School of Marine and Atmospheric Science, or the Scripps Institution of Oceanography in California, you should plan to spend some time learning about their activities and studying their exhibits.

Volunteer work for students is often available with research teams, nonprofit organizations, and public centers such as aquariums. If you do not live near water, try to find summer internships, camps, or programs that involve travel to a coastal area.

EMPLOYERS

At present, the government employs approximately 23 percent of oceanographers. Another 40 percent hold academic positions. The remainder work for private industry and not-for-profit environmental organizations.

Within the federal government, oceanographers are employed by the National Science Foundation; Departments of Commerce (National Oceanic and Atmospheric Administration), Defense, Energy, and Interior (National Park Service, Minerals Management Service); National Aeronautics and Space Administration; Environmental Protection Agency; Biological Resources Discipline of the U.S. Geological Survey; Naval Oceanographic Office; Naval Research Laboratory; and Office of Naval Research.

Private sector oceanographers may be engaged in research and development or resource management. For example, a biological oceanographer might work for a pharmaceutical company, trying to identify chemicals that could lead to the development of new medicines.

While positions in private industry tend to offer higher compensation than academic or governmental positions, industry scientists are expected to study topics of concern to their employer. Oceanographers who work for universities usually have more freedom to pursue the questions and ideas that interest them.

STARTING OUT

New graduates can obtain job leads from professors, contacts made through internships, or through their college's career services office. Additionally, the Marine Technology Society, American Society of Limnology and Oceanography, and The Oceanography Society offer job listings at their Web sites.

ADVANCEMENT

People who bring only a bachelor's degree will find themselves competing with oceanography graduate students for a limited number of technical assistant positions. The work can be interesting, often requiring sojourns at sea, but the opportunities for advancement are limited. Individuals who are not interested in conducting oceanographic research, however, may build rewarding careers designing or selling oceanographic equipment, advising industry, or developing communications materials for environmental organizations. Such positions may lead to opportunities in middle or upper management.

Most research and teaching positions are reserved for oceanographers with doctoral degrees. Oceanographers who complete a doctorate usually begin their careers in postdoctoral positions, assisting experienced oceanographers with research projects. After gaining two or three years of experience, an individual may become an assistant professor or assistant scientist. As such, the oceanographer may continue to assist more experienced scientists, and also assume teaching responsibilities. After establishing credentials as a knowledgeable, creative scientist, an oceanographer may begin to conduct his or her own research projects.

Experienced oceanographers usually can receive promotions and earn higher salaries by assuming administrative responsibilities.

EARNINGS

Salaries for biological oceanographers depend on education, experience, and other factors.

According to the U.S. Department of Labor, in 2009, salaries for geoscientists (an occupational group that includes geologists, geophysicists, and oceanographers) ranged from less than $43,140 to more than $161,260, with a median of $81,220. The average salary for experienced oceanographers working for the federal government was $105,671 in 2009.

Benefits for oceanographers include vacation and sick time, health, and sometimes dental, insurance, and pension or 401(k) plans. Self-employed oceanographers must provide their own benefits. In addition to their regular salaries, they also supplement their incomes with fees earned from lecturing, consulting, and publishing their findings.

WORK ENVIRONMENT

Biological oceanographers work in comfortable, well-lit offices and laboratories. They also work in the field on research vessels or research stations in sometimes inhospitable locales such as the Arctic. The work environment can be extremely hot, cold, windy, rainy, or snowy. Biological oceanographers who conduct field research are away from their friends and families for a few days or months at a time and live in cramped quarters on research vessels or in shoreline facilities with other marine scientists. Biological oceanographers must be able to tolerate sea travel; people who suffer from seasickness may want to think twice about choosing a career in seagoing oceanography. (It is important to note that many career paths in oceanography don't involve going to sea.)

Biological oceanographers who work in academic settings such as colleges and high schools enjoy the benefits of the academic calendar, with breaks and summer vacations allowing for research and travel.

OUTLOOK

The U.S. Department of Labor predicts that employment for all geoscientists (including biological oceanographers) will grow faster than the average for all occupations through 2018. Funding for graduate students and professional positions is expected to increase during the coming decade in the areas of global climate change, environmental research and management, fisheries science, and marine biomedical and pharmaceutical research programs. Despite this prediction, competition for top positions will be strong. Biological oceanographers who have Ph.D.'s, speak a foreign language, and who are willing to work abroad will have especially strong employment prospects.

FOR MORE INFORMATION

For education and career information, contact the following organizations:

Acoustical Society of America
Two Huntington Quadrangle, Suite 1NO1
Melville, NY 11747-4502
Tel: 516-576-2360
E-mail: asa@aip.org
http://asa.aip.org

American Geophysical Union
2000 Florida Avenue, NW
Washington, DC 20009-1277
Tel: 800-966-2481
http://www.agu.org

This organization for diving scientists stresses diving safety and offers internships for college students.

American Academy of Underwater Sciences
Dauphin Island Sea Lab
101 Bienville Boulevard
Dauphin Island, AL 36528-4603
Tel: 251-591–3775
E-mail: aaus@disl.org
http://www.aaus.org

For information on fisheries science, contact

American Fisheries Society
5410 Grosvenor Lane
Bethesda, MD 20814-2144
Tel: 301-897-8616
http://www.fisheries.org

The Education section of the institute's Web site has information on careers in biology.

American Institute of Biological Sciences
1444 I Street, NW, Suite 200
Washington, DC 20005-6535

Tel: 202-628-1500
http://www.aibs.org

Visit the society's Web site for information on careers and education.
American Society of Limnology and Oceanography
5400 Bosque Boulevard, Suite 680
Waco, TX 76710-4446
Tel: 800-929-2756
E-mail: business@aslo.org
http://www.aslo.org

For links to career information and sea programs, visit the follow-ing Web sites:
Careers in Oceanography, Marine Science, and Marine Biology
http://ocean.peterbrueggeman.com/career.html

Sea Grant Marine Careers
http://www.marinecareers.net

WomenOceanographers.org
http://www.womenoceanographers.org

For information about careers, educational programs, scholarships, and student competitions, contact
Marine Technology Society
5565 Sterrett Place, Suite 108
Columbia, MD 21044-2606
Tel: 410-884-5330
http://www.mtsociety.org

For information on oceanography, contact
National Oceanic and Atmospheric Administration
U.S. Department of Commerce
1401 Constitution Avenue, NW, Room 5128
Washington, DC 20230-0001
http://www.noaa.gov

Contact the society for ocean news and information on membership.
The Oceanography Society
PO Box 1931
Rockville, MD 20849-1931
Tel: 301-251-7708
E-mail: info@tos.org
http://www.tos.org

For information on diving instruction and certification, contact
Professional Association of Diving Instructors (PADI)
30151 Tomas Street
Rancho Santa Margarita, CA 92688-2125
Tel: 800-729-7234
http://www.padi.com

INTERVIEW

*Dr. Pamela Hallock-Muller is a professor of biogeological ocean-
ography at the University of South Florida. She discussed the field
with the editors of* Careers in Focus: Oceanography.

Q. What is biogeological oceanography?

A. The best way to understand a term like *biogeological oceanography* is to break it down into its parts. *Oceanography* is the
scientific study of the oceans and can include any aspect of the
oceans, including ocean water, the ocean floor, and life in the
oceans. In reality, oceanography and marine science are essen-
tially the same scientific discipline, although oceanography has
tended to be more focused on the open ocean while marine
science has tended to focus more on coastal waters. Geological oceanography, also known as marine geology, is the science
of the ocean floor, including the structure and makeup of the
seafloor, continental shelves and coastlines, and the history
of the evolution of those features over time. Because roughly
half the seafloor overall is covered by sediment particles that
originated from the shells or skeletons of tiny marine creatures,
the study of ocean sediments requires an understanding of the
biology of the creatures whose shells make up those sediments,
and therefore involves the study of biological oceanography.
Biogeological oceanographers use biology in their study of geological problems and questions, and geology, which includes
paleontology, in researching biological questions. I personally
study coral reefs, including the ecology of organisms living on
the reefs, the sediment and reef structures produced by the
shells and skeletons of those organisms, and how those organisms and ecological processes change over time.

**Q. What is one thing that young people may not know about
this discipline and a career in the field?**

A. One thing that young people often do not know about oceanography and marine science is that this field is inherently

interdisciplinary. Most people, both youngsters and adults, equate oceanography and marine science with "marine biology," and do not realize that there are lots of great careers for persons who love chemistry, physics, math, or geology, not just for "marine biologists." In fact, math, physics, and chemistry are essential tools for marine biologists, marine geologists, and biogeological oceanographers.

Q. What are some of the pros and cons of your job?

A. I am a university professor in the College of Marine Science; I love almost everything about my job except meetings and paperwork. I love learning and discovering. I enjoy thinking about research ideas and planning research projects. I love doing field research, which often includes travel to interesting places. I love collecting and analyzing data. And I love writing up my data and ideas into research papers that are published. And I enjoy presenting those ideas and results in talks. I also enjoy teaching classes, because I often learn as much from teaching as my students learn—sometimes more. I enjoy working with my graduate students and seeing them develop into scientists.

One thing I don't enjoy is struggling to get funding to support my graduate students and carry out our research, because no matter how good the idea or well written the proposal, it still has only about a one in 10 chance of getting funded. Another thing I don't enjoy is faculty or committee meetings where things are discussed that have been discussed many times before and there is no hope of ever making things better because the university administration or the legislature or some power beyond our control is making decisions that make doing our job more difficult. Something equivalent to such meetings is a fact of life in almost any field.

Q. What are the most important personal and professional qualities for biogeological oceanographers?

A. The most important personal and professional qualities for biogeological oceanographers are curiosity, integrity, perseverance, and an open mind. I have a poster on my wall that says, "Minds are like parachutes, they only function when open." It also helps if you like looking through microscopes at interesting things!

Q. What activities would you suggest to high school students who are interested in this career?

A. I am going to break this into two categories: academic preparation and outside activities:

Essential academic preparation for any science, from biogeological oceanography to veterinary medicine, includes all the mathematics and language arts possible, because mathematics, speaking, and writing are tools that you will use every day of your working life. At the high school level, mathematics and the language arts are more important than specific science courses; science courses keep one interested in moving forward, but mastering the math and language tools early will be infinitely helpful in mastering the sciences when one moves on to college.

Outside activities that can be useful for high school students include participating in mathematics, speech and writing contests, science fairs and bowls, athletics, and other activities that teach both teamwork and grace in losing when you have done your best. Useful volunteer and personal activities can be anything that gets one outside to see, observe, and appreciate nature. Bird-watching and insect or shell collecting are activities that teach observation and appreciation for nature and biological diversity. And reading—especially reading popular science articles or books and biographies of scientists!

Q. What is the future employment outlook for biogeological oceanographers?

A. The single greatest advantage of training in biogeological oceanography is that it is so interdisciplinary that one has great flexibility of skills and knowledge. As a result, career opportunities can range from teaching and research, to environmental management, to resource exploration and exploitation. Some of the things my former students are doing [this year] include studying coastal erosion in Alaska and coral reefs in Australia, Florida, Samoa, and around the Caribbean; managing coastal resources and alternative energy development; working with artificial intelligence; researching natural products to find cures for diseases; working for oil companies; teaching; and working for or owning/operating marine-related businesses.

Q. What has been one of your most rewarding experiences in your career and why?

A. My most rewarding career experience occurs every time one of my graduate students successfully defends a master's thesis or doctoral dissertation.

Chemical Oceanographers

QUICK FACTS

School Subjects
Biology
Chemistry

Personal Skills
Communication/ideas
Technical/scientific

Work Environment
Indoors and outdoors
One location with some
 travel

Minimum Education Level
Bachelor's degree

Salary Range
$43,140 to $81,220 to
$161,260+

Certification or Licensing
Voluntary

Outlook
Faster than the average

DOT
024

GOE
02.03.03

NOC
2113

O*NET-SOC
19-2042.00

OVERVIEW

Oceanographers obtain scientific information about the ocean through observations, surveys, and experiments. *Chemical oceanographers* are specialized oceanographers who investigate the chemical composition of the water and ocean floor. They study seawater components, pollutants, and trace chemicals, which are small amounts of dissolved substances that give an area of water a specific quality.

HISTORY

Our world's oceans have been observed and studied for thousands of years by mariners, explorers, and scientists.

One of the first great ocean expeditions was conducted by the HMS *Challenger* from 1872–76. The expedition, under the leadership of British naturalist John Murray and Scottish naturalist Charles Wyville Thomson, traveled to every ocean except the Arctic to collect samples and specimens, take depth soundings, record water temperatures, and conduct other research. The expedition helped scientists learn more about the world's oceans than was ever known.

From 1925 to 1927, a German research expedition aboard the *Meteor* studied the physical oceanography of the Atlantic Ocean. This expedition marked the beginning of the modern age of oceanographic investigation, according to *Invitation to Oceanography,* by Paul R. Pinet.

Scientists continued to study the world's oceans for the next three decades, but it was not until the 1960s and 1970s that technology and science advanced sufficiently to allow complex chemical analyses of the oceans. Today, these advances are allowing chemical oceanographers to conduct research that helps us understand the chemical makeup of the oceans and global warming, pollution, and other man-made and natural developments.

THE JOB

Chemical oceanographers study the chemical characteristics of the ocean and the chemical interactions that occur between the ocean, the atmosphere, and the sea floor. They study the impact these chemical interactions have on living organisms and man-made materials. They study the effects of pollution (runoff of sewage, oil, fuel, and agricultural chemicals) on the ocean. For example, a chemical oceanographer employed by the Environmental Protection Agency might conduct research to identify toxic compounds in sediments gathered from the ocean floor. Once the toxic compound is pinpointed, it can be traced to its source (illegal chemical dumping, etc.) and future pollution can be prevented. Other chemical oceanographers are studying carbon cycling in the world's oceans. This research helps scientists determine the degree and speed of global warming and its effects on ocean environments and human populations. One major recent focus of chemical oceanographers is on the role seawater temperature and salinity play in global climate change. Chemical oceanographers also may investigate ocean resources that may be useful for fuel, food, or medicine.

Chemical oceanographers use a variety of techniques to study the chemical makeup of oceans, including underwater mass spectrometry, fluorescence techniques, laser methods, high performance liquid chromatography, stable isotope mass spectrometry, radionuclide counting, high resolution gas chromatography, and combined gas chromatography-mass spectrometry. They also use computers to record their data and mathematical modeling software to test their hypotheses and come to conclusions about research topics.

Chemical oceanography is a highly interdisciplinary field. Chemical oceanographers work closely with oceanographers in other specialties, marine engineers, chemists, biologists, biochemists, and other marine scientists.

There are several subspecialties in the field of chemical oceanography. *Marine chemists* study the past and current chemical composition of seawater. They try to protect the oceans from pollution and seek out ocean resources that may have medicinal properties. *Marine geochemists* are concerned with the chemical composition of, and the changes in, minerals and rocks. They also study the role that organisms play in the formation and changing of geological features. *Marine biogeochemists* study the geological, physical, and biological processes that fuel chemical cycling in ocean systems. *Atmospheric chemists* study chemicals in the atmosphere and their relationship with the oceans.

Many chemical oceanographers are employed at colleges and universities. They teach classes and conduct research in laboratories and in the field. Some write textbooks and articles about the field.

REQUIREMENTS

High School
You will need a college degree to work as an oceanographer so be sure to take four years of college preparatory courses while in high school. Math classes, such as algebra, trigonometry, calculus, and statistics, and science courses, including chemistry, biology, and geology, are especially important to take. Take English and speech to help you hone your writing and oral communication skills. Computer classes will also be useful. Oceanographers use computers and other technology to conduct research, record their findings, and test their hypotheses. Taking a foreign language will also be useful— especially for those who plan to work abroad.

Postsecondary Training
A bachelor's degree is the minimum educational requirement to enter the field, but most employers require a master's degree in oceanography, chemistry, marine science, or a related field. Many chemical oceanographers earn bachelor's degrees in chemistry, biology, biochemistry, environmental toxicology, or a related field before continuing their education to earn a graduate degree in oceanography. As a college student preparing for graduate work in chemical oceanography, you should take mathematics through differential and integral calculus and at least one year each of physics, biology or geology, and a modern foreign language. In addition, you should include courses in field research or laboratory work in oceanography where available.

A Ph.D. in oceanography is required for most positions in research and teaching. More than 100 institutions offer programs in marine studies, and more than 35 universities have graduate programs leading to a doctoral degree in oceanography.

Typical classes in a chemical oceanography program include Methods in Chemical Oceanography, Marine Pollution, Marine

Organic Chemistry, Basic Clean Room Techniques, Applications of Gas Chromatography Mass Spectrometry, Petroleum Geochemistry, Chemical Oceanography Laboratory, Marine Pollution, Aquatic Radiogeochemistry, and Special Topics in Chemical Oceanography.

Many oceanography students participate in internships or work as teaching assistants while in college to gain hands-on experience in the field. A list of internships can be found at the American Society of Limnology and Oceanography's Web site, http://www.aslo.org.

Certification or Licensing

Oceanographers may scuba dive when conducting research. Organizations such as PADI provide basic certification (see For More Information for contact details).

Other Requirements

Chemical oceanographers should have a strong interest in science (especially chemistry), enjoy conducting research and solving problems, have an interest in working outdoors in all types of weather, and be able to work as a member of a team. They should also have excellent communication skills in order to interact well with coworkers and convey their findings in oral and written form. Other important skills include integrity, perseverance, open-mindedness, and attention to detail.

EXPLORING

Read books and visit Web sites about general oceanography and the specialization of chemical oceanography. One book suggestion: *Chemical Oceanography*, 3d ed., by Frank J. Millero. You can also visit Sea Grant's Marine Careers Web site (http://www.marinecareers.net) for information on careers, internships, volunteerships, and other activities, such as sea camps. You should also visit the Web sites of college oceanography departments to learn about typical classes, degree requirements, and internships. You may even be able to contact a professor or department head to ask a few questions about the career. If you are unable to contact, a professor, ask your high school counselor to arrange an information interview with a chemical oceanographer.

Visiting oceanography research centers, such as Woods Hole Oceanographic Institution on Cape Cod, the University of Miami's Rosenstiel School of Marine and Atmospheric Science, or the Scripps Institution of Oceanography in California, is another excellent way to learn more about the field. If you don't live near a coastal region, you can instead visit a local aquarium or even a zoo to learn about ocean environments or try to find summer internships, camps, or programs that involve travel to a coastal area.

EMPLOYERS

Chemical oceanographers are employed by state and federal governments agencies (such as the Environmental Protection Agency, the Biological Resources Discipline of the U.S. Geological Survey, and the National Oceanic and Atmospheric Administration), colleges and universities, private industries such as oil and gas extraction and pharmaceutical companies, and nonprofit environmental organizations.

An increasing number of oceanographers are being employed each year by industrial firms, particularly those involved in oceanographic instrument and equipment manufacturing, shipbuilding, and chemistry.

STARTING OUT

Many oceanography graduates obtain their first job in the field as a result of contacts made during internships and related opportunities with government agencies or private industry during college. College career services offices can also provide job leads. Additionally, the Marine Technology Society, American Society of Limnology and Oceanography, and The Oceanography Society provide job listings at their Web sites.

ADVANCEMENT

Chemical oceanographers advance by receiving recognition for their work, obtaining employment at larger companies or government agencies, working on more advanced research projects, or, if they are teachers, advancing up the academic ladder from instructor to assistant professor, to associate professor, to full professor. Some oceanographers may plan and supervise research projects involving a number of workers, or they may supervise an aquarium or oceanographic laboratory. Others become involved in marine policy planning and policymaking or policy interpretation.

EARNINGS

According to the U.S. Department of Labor, in 2009, salaries for geoscientists (an occupational group that includes geologists, geophysicists, and oceanographers) ranged from less than $43,140 to more than $161,260, with a median of $81,220. The average salary for experienced oceanographers working for the federal government was $105,671 in 2009.

Oceanographers usually receive good benefits, such as health insurance and retirement plans. In addition to their regular salaries, they also supplement their incomes with fees earned from consulting, lecturing, and publishing their findings.

WORK ENVIRONMENT

Chemical oceanographers in shore stations, laboratories, and research centers work five-day, 40-hour weeks. Occasionally, they serve a longer shift, particularly when a research experiment demands around-the-clock surveillance. Such assignments may also involve unusual working hours, depending on the nature of the research or the purpose of the trip. Trips at sea mean time away from home for periods extending from a few days to several months. Sea expeditions may be physically demanding and present an entirely different way of life: living on board a ship. Weather conditions may impose some hazards during these assignments. Choosing to engage in underwater research may mean a more adventuresome and hazardous way of life than in other occupations. It is wise to discover early whether or not life at sea appeals to you so that you may pursue appropriate jobs within the oceanography field.

Many jobs in oceanography, however, exist in laboratories, offices, and aquariums, with little time spent underwater or at sea. Many oceanographers are needed to analyze samples brought to land from sea; to plan, develop, and organize seafaring trips from land; and to teach. Oceanographers who work in colleges or universities get the added benefit of the academic calendar, which provides time off for travel or research.

OUTLOOK

The U.S. Department of Labor predicts that employment for all geoscientists (including chemical oceanographers) will grow faster than the average for all occupations through 2018. Chemical oceanographers will continue to play an important role in the field of marine science. They will be relied on to study the world's oceans to help reduce pollution, investigate how global warming and climate change are affecting the oceans, and help locate new sources of fuel, food, and medicine. Despite this prediction, competition for top positions will be strong. Opportunities will be best for those with

advanced degrees, proficiency in a foreign language, and a willingness to travel abroad.

FOR MORE INFORMATION

*This organization for diving scientists stresses diving safety and
offers internships for college students.*
   American Academy of Underwater Sciences
   Dauphin Island Sea Lab
   101 Bienville Boulevard
   Dauphin Island, AL 36528-4603
   Tel: 251-861-7504
   E-mail: aaus@disl.org
   http://www.aaus.org

*For general information about chemistry careers and approved edu-
cation programs, contact*
   American Chemical Society
   1155 16th Street, NW
   Washington, DC 20036-4839
   Tel: 800-227-5558
   E-mail: help@acs.org
   http://www.chemistry.org

Visit the society's Web site for information on careers and education.
   American Society of Limnology and Oceanography
   5400 Bosque Boulevard, Suite 680
   Waco, TX 76710-4446
   Tel: 800-929-2756
   E-mail: business@aslo.org
   http://www.aslo.org

*For links to career information and sea programs, visit the follow-
ing Web sites:*
   Careers in Oceanography, Marine Science, and Marine Biology
   http://ocean.peterbrueggeman.com/career.html

   Sea Grant Marine Careers
   http://www.marinecareers.net

   WomenOceanographers.org
   http://www.womenoceanographers.org

For information about careers, educational programs, scholarships, and student competitions, contact
Marine Technology Society
5565 Sterrett Place, Suite 108
Columbia, MD 21044-2606
Tel: 410-884-5330
http://www.mtsociety.org

For information on oceanography, contact
National Oceanic and Atmospheric Administration
U.S. Department of Commerce
1401 Constitution Avenue, NW, Room 5128
Washington, DC 20230-0001
http://www.noaa.gov

Contact the society for ocean news and information on membership.
The Oceanography Society
PO Box 1931
Rockville, MD 20849-1931
Tel: 301-251-7708
E-mail: info@tos.org
http://www.tos.org

For information on diving instruction and certification, contact
Professional Association of Diving Instructors (PADI)
30151 Tomas Street
Rancho Santa Margarita, CA 92688-2125
Tel: 800-729-7234
http://www.padi.com

College Professors, Oceanography/ Marine Science

QUICK FACTS

School Subjects
Biology
Earth science
Speech

Personal Skills
Communication/ideas
Helping/teaching

Work Environment
Indoors and outdoors
One location with some
travel

Minimum Education Level
Master's degree

Salary Range
$43,350 to $78,660 to
$133,080+

Certification or Licensing
None available

Outlook
Faster than the average

DOT
090

GOE
12.03.02

NOC
4121

O*NET-SOC
25-1051.00

OVERVIEW

College oceanography/marine science professors instruct undergraduate and graduate students about oceanography, marine science, and related subjects at colleges and universities. They lecture classes, supervise labs, and create and grade examinations. They also may conduct field research, write for publication, and aid in administration. Approximately 9,900 postsecondary atmospheric, earth, marine, and space sciences teachers are employed in the United States.

HISTORY

The concept of colleges and universities goes back many centuries. These institutions evolved slowly from monastery schools, which trained a select few for certain professions, notably theology. The terms *college* and *university* have become virtually interchangeable in America outside the walls of academia, although originally they designated two very different kinds of institutions.

Two of the most notable early European universities were the University of Bologna in Italy and the University of Paris. The University of Bologna was thought to have been established in the 12th century and the University of Paris was chartered in 1201. These universities were considered to be models after which other European universities were patterned. Oxford University in England was probably established during the 12th

42

century. Oxford served as a model for early American colleges and universities and today is still considered one of the world's leading institutions.

Harvard, the first U.S. college, was established in 1636. Its stated purpose was to train men for the ministry. All of the early colleges were established for religious training. With the growth of state-supported institutions in the early 18th century, the process of freeing the curriculum from ties with the church began. The University of Virginia established the first liberal arts curriculum in 1825, and these innovations were later adopted by many other colleges and universities.

Although the original colleges in the United States were patterned after Oxford University, they later came under the influence of German universities. During the 19th century, more than 9,000 Americans went to Germany to study. The emphasis in German universities was on the scientific method. Most of the people who had studied in Germany returned to the United States to teach in universities, bringing this objective, factual approach to education, the sciences (including chemistry, biology, and mathematics), and other fields of learning.

Oceans and marine life have been studied since ancient times. In fact, *Historia Animalium,* the first treatise on marine biology, was written by the philosopher Aristotle in 325 B.C.

In the United States, the study of the oceans began in force in the late 1800s, with the establishment of the U.S. Fish Commission (1871); the Anderson School of Natural History, the first U.S. marine station (1873); and the Marine Biological Laboratory (1888).

In 1903, the Scripps Institution of Biological Research (now known as the Scripps Institution of Oceanography) was founded at LaJolla, California, to conduct research on ocean life and educate students. Woods Hole Oceanographic Institution was founded at Cape Cod, Massachusetts, in 1930. Today, these schools are probably the best-known academic institutions in the United States that offer training in oceanography and marine science.

Oceanography education was buoyed by the passage of the Sea Grant College and Programs Act in 1966. The act provided nonmilitary funding for research and education in the marine sciences. With new funding available, more colleges and universities established marine science programs. Today, oceanography/marine science is a popular field of study at U.S. colleges and universities.

THE JOB

College and university faculty members teach oceanography, marine science, or related subjects at junior colleges or at four-year colleges and universities. At four-year institutions, most faculty members are *assistant professors, associate professors,* or *full professors.* These three types of professorships differ in regards to status, job responsibilities, and salary. Assistant professors are new faculty members who are working to get tenure (status as a permanent professor); they seek to advance to associate and then to full professorships.

College oceanography/marine science professors perform three main functions: teaching, service, and research. Their most important responsibility is to teach students. Their role within the department will determine the level of courses they teach and the number of courses per semester. Most professors work with students at all levels, from college freshmen to graduate students. They may teach several classes a semester or only a few a year. Though professors may spend only 12 to 16 hours a week in the actual classroom, they spend many hours preparing lesson plans, grading assignments and exams, and preparing grade reports. They also schedule office or laboratory hours during the week to be available to students outside of regular classes, and they meet with students individually throughout the semester. Many professors also work in the field as practicing oceanographers or marine scientists.

In the classroom, oceanography/marine science professors teach classes in one of the four main branches of the profession: biological oceanography, physical oceanography, chemical oceanography, and geological oceanography. In actual work, however, there is a tremendous amount of overlap between the four branches. Biological oceanography is the study of all aspects of the ocean's plant and animal life. Physical oceanography is the study of physical aspects of the ocean such as temperature and density, waves and currents, and the relationship between the ocean and the atmosphere. Chemical oceanography is the study of the chemical composition of the water and ocean floor. Geological oceanography is the study of the topographic features and physical composition of the ocean bottom. In addition, some professors may teach courses in ocean engineering, marine public policy, marine meteorology, and other ocean-related fields.

In addition to teaching classes, professors also administer exams and assign textbook reading and other research. In some courses, professors rely heavily on laboratories or field experiences to transmit course material.

An important part of teaching is advising students. Not all oceanography/marine science professors serve as advisers, but those who do must set aside large blocks of time to guide students through the program. College professors who serve as advisers may have any number of students assigned to them, from fewer than 10 to more than 100, depending on the administrative policies of the college. Their responsibility may involve looking over a planned program of studies to make sure the students meet requirements for graduation, or it may involve working intensively with each student on many aspects of college life. They may also discuss the different fields of oceanography and marine science with students and help them identify the best career choices.

All college professors provide important services to their department, college, or profession. Many college professors edit technical journals, review research and scholarship, and head committees about their field of expertise. College professors also serve on committees that determine the curriculum or make decisions about student learning.

The third responsibility of oceanography/marine science professors is research and publication. Faculty members who are heavily involved in research programs sometimes are assigned a smaller teaching load. College oceanography/marine science professors publish their research findings in various scholarly journals, including *Limnology and Oceanography* and *Oceanography.* They also write books based on their research or on their own knowledge and experience in the field. Most textbooks are written by college and university professors.

Publishing a significant amount of work has been the traditional standard by which assistant oceanography/marine science professors prove themselves worthy of becoming permanent, tenured faculty. Typically, pressure to publish is greatest for assistant professors. Pressure to publish increases again if an associate professor wishes to be considered for a promotion to full professorship. Professors in junior colleges face less pressure to publish than those in four-year institutions.

Some faculty members eventually rise to the position of *oceanography/marine science department chair,* where they govern the affairs of the entire department. Department chairs, faculty, and other professional staff members are aided in their myriad duties by *graduate assistants,* who may help develop teaching materials, conduct research, give examinations, teach lower level courses, and carry out other activities.

Some college oceanography/marine science professors may also conduct classes in an extension program. In such a program, they teach evening and weekend courses for the benefit of people who otherwise would not be able to take advantage of the institution's resources. They may travel away from the campus and meet with a group of students at another location. They may work full time for the extension division or may divide their time between on-campus and off-campus teaching.

Distance learning programs, an increasingly popular option for students, give oceanography/marine science professors the opportunity to use today's technologies to remain in one place while teaching students who are at a variety of locations simultaneously. The professor's duties, like those when teaching correspondence courses conducted by mail, include grading work that students send in at periodic intervals and advising students of their progress. Computers, the Internet, e-mail, and video conferencing, however, are some of the technology tools that allow professors and students to communicate in "real time" in a virtual classroom setting. Meetings may be scheduled during the same time as traditional classes or during evenings and weekends. Professors who do this work are sometimes known as *extension work, correspondence, online,* or *distance learning instructors.* They may teach online courses in addition to other classes or may have distance learning as their major teaching responsibility.

The *junior college instructor* has many of the same kinds of responsibilities as does the professor in a four-year college or university. Because junior colleges offer only a two-year program, they teach only undergraduates.

REQUIREMENTS
High School
Your high school's college preparatory program likely includes courses in English, science (especially oceanography, marine science, and other environment-related courses), foreign language, history, math, and government. In addition, you should take courses in speech to get a sense of what it will be like to lecture to a group of students. Your school's debate team can also help you develop public speaking skills, along with research skills.

Postsecondary Training
At least one advanced degree in oceanography, marine science, or a related field is required to be a professor in a college or university. The master's degree is considered the minimum standard, and graduate work beyond the master's is usually desirable to teach in most junior colleges. For those planning to teach in a four-year university, a Ph.D. is generally required. If you hope to advance in academic rank above instructor, most institutions require a doctorate.

In the last year of your undergraduate program, you'll apply to graduate programs in your area of study. Standards for admission to a graduate program can be high and the competition heavy, depend-

A marine biology professor works with a student to examine microbiological samples collected from ocean bays as part of their study of marine ecosystems. *(James Marshall, The Image Works)*

ing on the school. Once accepted into a program, your responsibilities will be similar to those of your professors—in addition to attending seminars, you'll research, prepare articles for publication, and teach some undergraduate courses.

You may find employment in a junior college with only a master's degree. Advancement in responsibility and in salary, however, is more likely to come if you have earned a doctorate.

Other Requirements

First and foremost, you should have a passion for oceanography and marine science and enjoy sharing this passion with others. You should also like to read, write, and conduct research. You will spend many years studying in school, and your whole career will be based on communicating your thoughts and ideas. People skills are important because you'll be dealing directly with students, administrators, and other faculty members on a daily basis. You should feel comfortable in a role of authority and possess self-confidence.

EXPLORING

Your high school teachers use many of the same skills as college professors, so talk to your teachers about their careers and their college experiences. You can develop your own teaching experience by volunteering at a community center, working at a day care center, or working at a summer camp (especially one that focuses on oceanography/marine science). Also, spend some time on a college campus to get a sense of the environment. Write to colleges for their admissions brochures and course catalogs (or check them out online); read about the faculty members in oceanography/marine science departments and the courses they teach. Before visiting college campuses, make arrangements to speak to professors who teach courses that interest you. These professors may allow you to sit in on their classes and observe. Also, make appointments with college advisers and with people in the admissions and recruitment offices. If your grades are good enough, you might be able to serve as a teaching assistant during your undergraduate years, which can give you experience leading discussions and grading papers.

EMPLOYERS

Approximately 9,900 postsecondary atmospheric, earth, marine, and space sciences teachers are employed in the United States. Employment opportunities vary based on area of study and education. With a doctorate, a number of publications, and a record of good teaching, professors should find opportunities in universities all across the country. Oceanography/marine science professors teach in undergraduate and graduate programs. The teaching jobs at doctoral institutions are usually better paying and more prestigious. The most sought-after positions are those that offer tenure. Teachers that have only a master's degree will be limited to opportunities with junior colleges, community colleges, and some small private institutions. The two largest academic employers of oceanographers are Woods Hole Oceanographic Institution and the Scripps Institution of Oceanography, though many coastal universities also maintain excellent oceanographic programs.

STARTING OUT

You should start the process of finding a teaching position while you are in graduate school. The process includes developing a curriculum vitae (a detailed, academic resume), writing for publication, assisting with research, attending conferences, and gaining teaching experience and recommendations. Many students begin applying for teaching positions while finishing their graduate program. For most positions at four-year institutions, you must travel to large conferences where interviews can be arranged with representatives from the universities to which you have applied.

Because of the competition for tenure-track positions, you may have to work for a few years in temporary positions, visiting various schools as an adjunct professor. Some professional associations maintain lists of teaching opportunities in their areas. They may also make lists of applicants available to college administrators looking to fill an available position.

ADVANCEMENT

The normal pattern of advancement is from instructor to assistant professor, to associate professor, to full professor. All four academic ranks are concerned primarily with teaching and research. College faculty members who have an interest in and a talent for administration may be advanced to chair of a department or to dean of their college. A few become college or university presidents or other types of administrators.

The instructor is usually an inexperienced college teacher. He or she may hold a doctorate or may have completed all the Ph.D. requirements except for the dissertation. Most colleges look upon the rank of instructor as the period during which the college is trying out the teacher. Instructors usually are advanced to the position of assistant professors within three to four years. Assistant professors are given up to about six years to prove themselves worthy of tenure, and if they do so, they become associate professors. Some professors choose to remain at the associate level. Others strive to become full professors and receive greater status, salary, and responsibilities.

Most colleges have clearly defined promotion policies from rank to rank for faculty members, and many have written statements about the number of years in which instructors and assistant professors may remain in grade. Administrators in many colleges hope to encourage younger faculty members to increase their skills and competencies and thus to qualify for the more responsible positions of associate professor and full professor.

EARNINGS

Earnings vary by the departments professors work in, by the size of the school, by the type of school (public, private, women's only, for example), and by the level of position the professor holds.

According to the U.S. Department of Labor, in 2009, the median salary for postsecondary atmospheric, earth, marine, and space sciences teachers was $78,660, with 10 percent earning $133,080 or more and 10 percent earning $43,350 or less. Atmospheric, earth, marine, and space sciences teachers employed at junior colleges had mean annual earnings of $73,900, and those employed at four-year universities earned $85,660. Those with the highest earnings tend to be senior tenured faculty; those with the lowest, graduate assistants. Professors working on the West Coast and the East Coast and those working at doctorate-granting institutions also tend to have the highest salaries. Many professors try to increase their earnings by completing research, publishing in their field, or teaching additional courses.

Benefits for full-time faculty typically include health insurance and retirement funds and, in some cases, stipends for travel related to research, housing allowances, and tuition waivers for dependents.

WORK ENVIRONMENT

A college or university is usually a pleasant place in which to work. Campuses bustle with all types of activities and events, stimulating ideas, and a young, energetic population. Much prestige comes with success as a professor and scholar; professors have the respect of students, colleagues, and others in their community.

Depending on the size of the department, college oceanography/marine science professors may have their own office, or they may have to share an office with one or more colleagues. Their department may provide them with a computer, Internet access, and research assistants. College professors are also able to do much of their office work at home. They can arrange their schedule around class hours, academic meetings, and the established office hours when they meet with students. Most college teachers work more than 40 hours each week. Although college professors may teach only two or three classes a semester, they spend many hours preparing for lectures, examining student work, and conducting research.

Academic positions usually entail a combination of teaching and research. Experienced oceanographers who work for large universities may devote the lion's share of their time to research, teaching only one or two classes each year. Oceanographers who teach at smaller institutions or at the undergraduate level, on the other hand, may be entirely occupied with teaching.

OUTLOOK

The U.S. Department of Labor predicts that employment for college and university professors will grow faster than the average for all careers through 2018. College enrollment is projected to grow due to an increased number of 18- to 24-year-olds, an increased number of adults returning to college, and an increased number of foreign-born students. Retirement of current faculty members will also provide job openings. However, competition for full-time, tenure-track positions at four-year schools will be very strong. More opportunities will be found at community colleges and in high schools.

There will be strong competition for positions as oceanography/marine science professors. Work in academia is appealing to many marine science professionals, and only those with Ph.D.'s and experience will be eligible for positions at top universities.

A number of factors threaten to change the way colleges and universities hire faculty. Some university leaders are developing more business-based methods of running their schools, focusing on profits and budgets. This can affect college professors in a number of ways. One of the biggest effects is in the replacement of tenure-track faculty positions with part-time instructors. These part-time instructors include adjunct faculty, visiting professors, and graduate students. Organizations such as the American Association of University Professors and the American Federation of Teachers are working to prevent the loss of these full-time jobs as well as to help part-time instructors receive better pay and benefits. Other issues involve the development of long-distance education departments in many schools. Though these correspondence courses have become very popular in recent years, many professionals believe that students in long-distance education programs receive only a second-rate education. A related concern is about the proliferation of computers in the classroom. Some courses consist only of instruction by computer software and the Internet. The effects of these alternative methods on the teaching profession will be offset somewhat by the expected increases in college enrollment in coming years.

FOR MORE INFORMATION

This organization for diving scientists stresses diving safety and offers internships for college students.
American Academy of Underwater Sciences
Dauphin Island Sea Lab
101 Bienville Boulevard
Dauphin Island, AL 36528-4603
Tel: 251-861-7504
E-mail: aaus@disl.org
http://www.aaus.org

To read about the issues affecting college professors, contact the following organizations:
American Association of University Professors
1133 19th Street, NW, Suite 200
Washington, DC 20036-3655
Tel: 202-737-5900
E-mail: aaup@aaup.org
http://www.aaup.org

American Federation of Teachers
555 New Jersey Avenue, NW
Washington, DC 20001-2029
Tel: 202-879-4400
http://www.aft.org

The association represents the interests of women in higher education. Visit its Web site for information on scholarships for college students and AAUW Outlook.
American Association of University Women (AAUW)
1111 16th Street, NW

Washington, DC 20036-4809
Tel: 800-326-2289
E-mail: connect@aauw.org
http://www.aauw.org

Visit the society's Web site for information on careers and education.
American Society of Limnology and Oceanography
5400 Bosque Boulevard, Suite 680
Waco, TX 76710-4446
Tel: 800-929-2756
E-mail: business@aslo.org
http://www.aslo.org

For information about careers, educational programs, scholarships, and student competitions, contact
Marine Technology Society
5565 Sterrett Place, Suite 108
Columbia, MD 21044-2606
Tel: 410-884-5330
http://www.mtsociety.org

For information on geoscience education, contact
National Association of Geoscience Teachers
c/o Carleton College B-SERC
One North College Street
Northfield, MN 55057-4001
Tel: 507-222-5634
http://nagt.org

For information about earth science, visit the association's Web site.
National Earth Science Teachers Association
http://www.nestanet.org

For information on marine education in all settings, contact
National Marine Educators Association
PO Box 1470
Ocean Springs, MS 39564-1470
Tel: 228-896-9182
http://www.marine-ed.org

For information on science education, contact
National Science Teachers Association
1840 Wilson Boulevard
Arlington VA 22201-3092

Tel: 703-243-7100
http://www.nsta.org

Contact the society for ocean news and information on membership for college students.
The Oceanography Society
PO Box 1931
Rockville, MD 20849-1931
Tel: 301-251-7708
E-mail: info@tos.org
http://www.tos.org

INTERVIEW

Piers Chapman is the head of the Department of Oceanography at Texas A&M University. He discussed the field with the editors of Careers in Focus: Oceanography.

Q. Can you please tell us about your program and internship opportunities that are available to students at your school?

A. The Department of Oceanography (OCNG) at Texas A&M University (TAMU) in College Station, Texas, offers primarily graduate degrees (M.S. and Ph.D.) in various aspects of oceanography (biological, chemical, geological, and physical). We do not have an undergraduate major in oceanography, because we believe that it is more important to gain a firm grounding in one of the basic sciences before switching to the marine realm. It is very hard, for instance, to get a degree in marine biology if you don't have a good background in biology; the same goes for chemical, geological, and physical oceanography. We do, however, offer a minor, which requires 15 credit hours, as well as various optional courses that can be used to complete the science requirements of TAMU.

Internships are not generally available to outsiders, but TAMU undergraduate students in any discipline can obtain research experience in several of the laboratories in the department. This is usually in summer, but vacancies can occur year round.

Q. Can you tell us a little about your background and how you entered the field?

A. My background is rather unusual, in that I was appointed as head of department at TAMU without ever having been a member of a faculty at a university. My first degree was in chemistry, at the University College of North Wales, Bangor, Wales. I then did a Ph.D. in marine chemistry at the marine laboratory at the same university, followed by a postdoctoral stint at the University of East Anglia, Norwich, England. So far, this is pretty normal. Most people who want to be university professors then get a position as an assistant professor and start working their way up the academic ladder. However, this isn't always necessary, and I went to work for a year doing analyses of drinking water, industrial wastewater, sewage effluents, and the Humber estuary for the U.K. Yorkshire Water Authority. The Humber work was particularly entertaining, as we did all the sampling by bucket from a helicopter hovering about 30 feet above the river.

After this I moved to Cape Town, South Africa, where I worked for the Sea Fisheries Research Institute as a marine chemist. The basic job of this government institute was to tell the responsible minister how to set the annual commercial fishing quotas, but we needed to do lots of research into the physical and chemical oceanography around the country to help the biologists with their mathematical models of fish stocks. It was a lot of fun going out on fishery cruises to do physical and chemical sampling of the water column when we weren't fishing (bottom and mid-water trawling), but there were also dedicated cruises for chemical and physical oceanography, and I usually managed two or three cruises per year. I also did quite a bit of work on marine pollution, particularly the problems of oil pollution around the coast resulting from accidents to both tankers (large-scale problems of up to 100,000 tons of crude oil) and fishing boats (smaller and more localized, usually about 200 tons of diesel fuel). In either case, it makes a mess.

In 1990, I arrived in College Station to run the U.S. Office of an international deep-sea oceanography program, the World Ocean Circulation Experiment. This involved me in lots of meetings, both within the United States and elsewhere around the world. About 25 nations were involved, and the field program went on from 1990 through about 1998, followed by an additional five years of analysis, interpretation, modeling, and synthesis. The data are still being used in research. The program included a large number of trans-ocean cruises, and I was able to take part in two of these, one from South America to Cape Town across the South Atlantic, the other in the Indian Ocean from Mauritius to Muscat (Oman), which involved an equator crossing and the initiation rites that go with this.

In 2002, I moved from Texas to Louisiana State University in Baton Rouge, Louisiana, where I set up a program in coastal restoration science for the National Oceanographic and Atmospheric Administration (NOAA). This program provided funding for university scientists doing research on how to reduce coastal erosion in Louisiana and Mississippi. I was then asked to apply for my present position within OCNG, and returned to TAMU in late 2007.

Currently, when not running the department here at TAMU, I'm working on the oceanography of the Gulf of Mexico and studying the low dissolved oxygen water mass that forms annually off the coast of Louisiana and Texas. During my career I have spent about two-and-a-half years at sea on research cruises, looking at different aspects of marine chemistry. These have varied from short trips of a few days close to the coast to longer, deepwater cruises of up to six weeks. I've worked around the United Kingdom and in the Bay of Biscay, all around South Africa and Namibia, including one trip to the Antarctic, in the Gulf of Mexico, and across the South Atlantic and in the Indian Ocean. It can be a great way to see the world!

Q. What are some things about oceanography that young people may not know?

A. As a career, oceanography is an unusual study area, in that it takes specialists from many fields, such as biology, chemistry, geology, mathematics, physics, geophysics, meteorology, or engineering and broadens their education. Most graduate degrees do the opposite. This is because much of oceanography requires interdisciplinary knowledge, with inputs from several different fields. Chemists, physical oceanographers, biologists, and geologists can all work on different parts of a common problem, and they frequently use mathematical models, which require advanced computing skills, to help them.

You may have seen the pale blue floats of the Portuguese Man o' War (*Physalia*) washed up on beaches after storms, and I hope you haven't been stung by their tentacles. (If you have been so unfortunate, use meat tenderizer to stop the pain; it breaks down the proteins that the animal injects). Did you know that these come in two mirror-image forms, which sail in opposite directions when the wind hits them?

Q. What advice would you give to high school students who are interested in this career?

A. Take whichever science classes provide a good background to the field of oceanography you are interested in. Also, take mathematics classes, including statistics; most universities insist that you pass calculus if you want to do any science degree, and oceanography is no exception as math is becoming more important in all fields of oceanography, including biology. A knowledge of statistics is also becoming more important. If you live in a coastal state or near the Great Lakes, there is an annual national competition, the National Ocean Sciences Bowl (http://www.oceanleadership.org/education/national-ocean-sciences-bowl), which is operated by the Consortium for Ocean Leadership (COL). Regional competitions are run by local universities under the overall management of COL. The competition is for high school teams, and the winners of the state competitions compete in the national final, usually in Washington, D.C. Prizes include trips to marine laboratories in places such as Hawaii or Alaska. Ask your science teachers to help you enter a team in this competition. You can also contact researchers at your local university; usually they are pleased to come and give talks at your school or to have interested students visit their laboratories.

Q. What are the most important professional qualities for oceanographers?

A. There is no professional association for oceanographers, although attempts are being made to start one. Since the field is so incredibly wide, I am not sure whether there is any need for one either. However, oceanographers need to show professionalism in their dealings with the rest of the community. One of the main requirements is probably the ability to analyze and draw conclusions from large and complicated data sets. Add to this the need to pay attention to detail, and good mathematical skills. As in all jobs, the ability to explain what you have done and why to people of all abilities, both by speaking and writing, is another asset. You may need to talk to farmers or fishermen one day, businessmen the next, and other oceanographers the day after.

Q. What is the future employment outlook in the field?

A. A lot of people go into oceanography with the intention of becoming university professors, but there are only a limited number of openings each year for such positions, and these days you almost certainly have to have a Ph.D. if you want to obtain one. However, there are also opportunities working for state and federal agencies, or private industry, and these positions may not require a Ph.D. Examples include the following:

- wildlife and fisheries programs, such as fisheries management or the National Park Service;
- other state and federal groups such as water and environmental quality departments or the Environmental Protection Agency and NOAA;
- aquaria and wildlife parks;
- aquaculture and food science;
- coastal zone management (becoming more important as we worry more about climate change and its associated problem of sea level rise);
- disaster relief (forecasting hurricane storm surges or oil spill trajectories);
- offshore oil and gas industry (both for physical oceanographers to look at winds, waves, and currents and chemists and geologists to help find new oil and gas deposits);
- port and harbor operators; and
- consulting companies.

Since Texas and the northern coast of the Gulf of Mexico is a major center for oil and gas exploration, industry has been looking for more and more oceanographers to assist companies in the complex aspects of finding oil and gas in deeper and deeper water (there are more than 4,000 wells in the northern Gulf and rigs are now operating many miles offshore and in water more than a mile deep). Unfortunately, the recent drop in the global oil price means that at present there is less demand for new graduates than there has been over the past few years, but assuming that the global economy picks up again, the price of a barrel of crude oil will almost certainly go up, too, which means more jobs at all levels in the industry.

Because oceanographers usually have good math skills and are often good at synthesizing large and complex data set, they can get well-paid jobs in other fields, such as banking. There are also careers in marine law, but here it is generally the legal side, rather than the oceanography, that is important.

Divers and Diving Technicians

OVERVIEW

Divers and diving technicians perform a wide variety of underwater jobs, both in oceans and in fresh water, using special underwater breathing equipment. The jobs include offshore oil well piping, scientific research, building and repair of foundations and other underwater construction, salvage work, and ship repair and service. Diving technicians may serve as "tenders," or support workers, for divers. They often act as intermediaries between administrative, scientific, or engineering staff and other skilled workers in a wide range of marine activities. They are expected to be familiar with the many aspects of diving and its related equipment and must also be able to perform numerous skills while underwater.

Many divers also work as *recreation specialists,* teaching diving classes to the general public and supervising diving activities for resorts and cruise ships.

HISTORY

Since earliest times, people have sought to go underwater to retrieve food or valuable items or to build and repair ships. Unfortunately, without equipment, a diver can stay under the surface only as long as a single breath allows. Other factors that limit the unaided diver's activities include cold water temperatures, the water pressure at great depths, and strong currents.

The first efforts to overcome these limitations with special equipment were primitive. To bring an air supply down, early divers used sections of hollow reeds as breathing tubes. The ancient Greeks used crude diving bells. But it was not until the late 18th century that a practical diving bell was invented. It allowed one person to descend into shallow water in an open-bottomed container supplied with air pumped by hand from above. In the 19th century, the first diving suit was devised, connected to the surface by a tube. Even with various improvements, however, diving suits were rather clumsy. In 1943, the invention of scuba (self-contained underwater breathing apparatus) equipment allowed divers more freedom of movement, opening up many new possibilities. Since then, diving techniques and equipment have become increasingly sophisticated.

The records of salvage from the Spanish galleon *Santa Margarita*, which sank in about 20 feet of water on the lower Florida Keys in 1622, tell something about the development of diving technology. In 1644, an effort was made to salvage the galleon's cargo of gold and silver. Diving crews, using a bronze bell as an air source, salvaged much of the silver coins and other items of value, but not the gold, which sank into the sand and could not be found. Some divers lost their lives, swept away by dangerous currents even in the shallow water.

In 1980, 336 years later, the wreck was found again. This time, diving teams used scuba equipment, electronic metal detectors, and special hydraulic jets that washed away the sand covering more than $20 million worth of gold and silver coins, ingots, gold chains, and other valuables. Modern equipment and techniques made all the difference.

One major problem with deepwater diving is caused by the additional pressure of the water's weight, which causes the nitrogen in the air breathed by the diver to dissolve in the bloodstream. Normally, the nitrogen remains in the lungs and is simply exhaled in the breathing process, but when a diver returns too rapidly from deep water to the surface, bubbles of nitrogen form in the blood vessels. These bubbles can cause serious sickness and even death. This condition is called the bends and is an ever-present hazard of deepwater diving. It can be prevented by making sure the diver returns slowly enough to the surface that the nitrogen in the blood is freed from the lungs and expelled normally, rather than forming bubbles in the blood vessels.

The U.S. Navy, which had a great amount of ship salvage and repair work to do during World War II, began to use new approaches to prevent the bends. A helium breathing mixture, instead of air, was proven to be safer and more efficient for deepwater divers. Divers who ascended too quickly were put in special decompression chambers.

Oceanography and Marine Science on the Web

Animal Corner
http://www.animalcorner.co.uk

Animal Diversity Web
http://animaldiversity.ummz.umich.edu

Animal Planet
http://animal.discovery.com

Association of Zoos and Aquariums
http://www.aza.org/ForEveryone/CareersKids

Careers in Aquatic and Marine Science
http://www.aqua.org/downloads/pdf/Marine_Science_
    Careers.pdf

Careers in Oceanography, Marine Science, and Marine Biology
http://ocean.peterbrueggeman.com/career.html

Magic Porthole
http://www.magicporthole.org

MarineBio
http://www.marinebio.com

Monterey Bay Aquarium: Science Careers
http://www.montereybayaquarium.org/lc/kids_place/kidseq_
    careers.asp

National Oceanic and Atmospheric Administration
http://www.noaa.gov

Preparing for a Wildlife Career
http://nationalzoo.si.edu/Education/WildlifeCareers

Sea Grant Marine Careers
http://www.marinecareers.net

Seaworld: Animals
http://www.seaworld.org

WomenOceanographers.org
http://www.womenoceanographers.org

Woods Hole Oceanographic Institution
http://www.whoi.edu

In the late 1950s and 1960s, underwater exploration increased. The depths of the oceans, which cover about 72 percent of the world's surface, were still the most uncharted part of the planet, presenting a challenge that, to many people, was comparable to exploring space. The growing offshore petroleum-drilling industry was another incentive to further develop diving technology. New kinds of diving bells, saturation diving systems, and a host of submersible devices allowed deeper and more effective underwater work, such as the 1985–86 exploration of the *Titanic* wreck several miles under the North Atlantic.

As diving and related activities came to involve more people and more complicated equipment, the need arose for workers who could handle many different kinds of technical tasks. Today, diving professionals are employed mainly in commercial diving; some work in marine science research and in recreational diving. Commercial diving relies on numerous mechanical, engineering, and construction skills transferred to an underwater setting. These jobs can be physically demanding and hazardous, but they also offer adventure and excitement.

THE JOB

Most job opportunities for divers and diving technicians are with commercial diving contractors. The work is frequently dirty, exhausting, and dangerous, and the duties vary greatly. Some common underwater jobs include inspecting structures or equipment using visual, photographic, or videotape methods; operating hand or power tools in mechanical construction or repair; cleaning marine growth from structures; welding or cutting in salvage, repair, or construction functions; and surveying for geological or biological research teams.

Diving technicians do not always work below the water; sometimes they work at the surface, as experts in the life-support system for divers and in the management of the equipment. These technicians work with the controls that supply the proper mixture of gases for the diver to breathe, maintain the correct pressures in the hoses leading to the underwater worker, and act as the communicator and life-support partner of the diver. They also monitor water depth, conditions inside diving bells and chambers, and decompression schedules for divers. This is a highly skilled position involving many responsibilities, and it is vital to the success of all deepwater diving operations.

It is possible in the future that the scientific and technological demands made on the life-support team may cause the development of a group of specialists who do not dive. However, the usual practice now is for divers to work both underwater and on deck.

Oceanographic research is another important employment specialty for divers and diving technicians. Diving professionals in this field help oceanographers and other marine scientists conduct research. They may operate underwater video, sonar, or other equipment to record marine life, underwater volcanoes, and other ocean phenomena. Some may repair or set up equipment on the ocean floor. Others may help construct underwater facilities used by marine scientists. Divers and diving technicians are also employed in undersea mining, oil and gas exploration, and underwater military engineering.

Some marine science diving professionals work as *diving safety officers*. These workers are employed by educational institutions such as the Scripps Institution of Oceanography to ensure that safety measures are observed by divers and diving technicians during scientific research expeditions. The diving safety officer trains divers and ensures that equipment is in good condition (and repairs it if it is not), that divers have regular physical examinations, and that dives follow the safety guidelines of the American Academy of Underwater Sciences. They often accompany scientists and the divers they supervise on expeditions that are conducted around the world. SanDiegoDiving.com estimates that there are only about 50 diving safety officers in the United States.

Divers and diving technicians also work as recreation specialists. They may be employed by dive resorts, dive charter boats, municipal recreation departments, dive stores, or postsecondary institutions. The work performed will vary depending on the employer's specific business, but it frequently includes teaching the general public about recreational diving, supervising and coordinating recreational dives at resorts and on cruise ships, teaching diving lessons and selling equipment at a retail dive store, and repairing equipment for customers of a dive store.

Newly hired technicians are normally assigned to organize the shop and care for and maintain all types of company equipment. Soon, they will be assigned a similar job on a diving boat or platform. When on a diving operation, technicians help maintain a safe and efficient operation by providing topside or surface support for the divers: they assist them with equipment, supply hoses, communications, necessary tools, and lines. As a diver's tender, technicians may monitor and control diving descent and ascent rates, breathing gas supplies, and decompression schedules. They must also be able to assist in an emergency and help treat a diver injured in an accident or suffering from the bends.

As technicians gain experience in company procedures and jobs, they are given more responsibility. Technicians usually can start underwater work within a few months to two years after being hired, depending on the technician's skills and the company's needs.

Technicians' first dives are shallow and relatively easy; subsequent dives match their ability and competence. With time and experience, they may advance to work deep-dive bell and saturation diving systems. Saturation divers are gradually compressed in an on-deck chamber, as they would be when diving, then transferred to and from the work site inside a pressurized bell. These divers stay in a pressure-controlled environment for extended periods.

All of the personnel on a diving crew should know how to care for and use a wide variety of equipment. Some of the commonly used diving equipment includes air compressors, decompression chambers, high-pressure breathing-gas storage tanks, pressure regulators and gas regulating systems, hoses and fittings for handling air and gas, and communications equipment.

A diver's personal equipment ranges from simple scuba, now seldom used, to full face masks; lightweight and heavy helmets for both air and helium/oxygen use; diving bells; and diving suits, from wet suits to the heavy dry suits that can be bolted to a breastplate to which the heavy helmet is attached. For cold water and deep or long-duration dives, a hot-water suit may be used. This allows a flow of warm water supplied from the surface to be passed through a loose-fitting wet suit on the diver's body, protecting the diver from body heat loss.

Commercial diving crews use simple hand tools, including hammers, crescent wrenches, screwdrivers, and pliers. Items such as wire cutters and volt/ohm meters are often needed. Divers should be versatile and may also be expected to use many types of power tools, as well as sophisticated and often delicate instruments, such as video and camera equipment, measuring instruments, ultrasonic probes, and metal detection devices. Knowledge of arc welding equipment and underwater arc or other metal-cutting equipment is very important for many kinds of work, such as salvage, construction, or repair and modification of underwater structures. These needs are often associated with underwater petroleum explorations, well-drilling operations, or management of piping systems.

Divers and diving technicians who work in marine science must be familiar with the use of basic research and recording equipment and scientific research techniques.

REQUIREMENTS

High School

Typical basic requirements for enrollment in a diving program are a high school diploma or its equivalent, reading comprehension, completion of three to four years of language and communications subjects, at least one year of algebra, and one year of physics or chemistry with laboratory work.

Postsecondary Training

The best way to train for this career is to attend one of the postsecondary schools and colleges that offer an organized program, usually two years in length, to prepare such technicians. Diving technicians are specialized engineering technicians. Therefore, you need a basic theoretical and practical background in science. Mastery of several construction-type work skills is also necessary. A typical postsecondary program in marine diving technology is designed to develop the skills and knowledge required of a commercial diver, an understanding of the marine environment, and an ability to communicate well.

The first year's study includes such courses as seamanship and small-boat handling, basic diving, drafting, basic welding, technical writing, advanced diving, fundamentals of marine engines and compressors, marine welding, physical oceanography, and marine biology. Often, students participate in a summer cooperative work-study program of supervised ocean dives before the second year of courses begins.

Second-year courses typically include underwater construction, biological oceanography, physics, fundamentals of electronics, machine shop operations, underwater operations, advanced diving systems, basic emergency medical technology, and speech and communications. The second year also may include fundamentals of photography or a special project that relates specifically to diving or life-support technology. Additional studies such as economics, American institutions, or other general studies must usually be taken.

Programs for prospective recreation specialists also focus on understanding the marine environment and developing communication skills, but instead of welding, drafting, and other technical classes, these programs require the development of basic business skills. Courses in small business management, introduction to marketing, organizational behavior, computer science, and business law are usually offered. Schools that provide these programs often have special admission requirements relating to swimming ability and skills.

When you seek employment, you usually find that many employers require completion of a recognized training program or documentation of comparable experience. Additionally, an emergency medical technician certificate is valuable and may be required by some companies.

Certification or Licensing
There are no special requirements for licenses at the entry level in the United States. However, the United Kingdom and some of the North Sea countries do have specific requirements for divers, which can be met only by training in their countries.

Certification is required for recreational diving instructors and is available through such organizations as NAUI Worldwide (formerly known as the National Association of Underwater Instructors), PADI, and the YMCA. Certification for commercial divers is not required.

For specific work beyond entry level, a welding certificate may be required. Also, a certification in nondestructive testing may enhance your opportunities. Both of these certificates are specific and beyond entry level. The employer will be able to specify the method of obtaining the special certificates they desire.

Other Requirements
Employment in areas other than commercial diving may impose more specific requirements. A specialty in photography, electronics, oceanography, biology, marine culture, or construction engineering may open other doors of opportunity for the diving technician.

You need more than excellent diving skills; diving is just the way they reach their work site. You should be mechanically inclined and able to operate and maintain a wide variety of equipment. You must understand drawings and simple blueprints; be familiar with piping and valves; know how to handle high-pressure gases, bottles, and gauges; and be able to write accurate reports, keep records, and do paperwork. An understanding of the physical and biological elements of the marine environment and the ability to work as a member of a team are crucial.

Recreation specialists need excellent communication skills. With some employers, business management, marketing, and computer skills are also important.

Physical requirements for the career include overall good health, at least normal physical strength, sound respiratory functions, normal or better eyesight, and good hand-eye coordination and manual dexterity.

EXPLORING

You can find information about training schools in trade journals and through professional associations. Libraries are a good place to look for program listings and descriptions. It is a good idea to contact several training programs and compare the offerings to your own individual needs. Make sure to ask about employment prospects for future graduates of each program.

A visit to one or more potential employers would certainly be of benefit. While observation of an offshore job would be difficult, a tour of the company shop, a look at its equipment, and a chance to talk to technicians should be informative and worthwhile.

Become proficient in scuba diving and outdoor swimming and diving. The experience of learning to feel at home in water and underwater not only can help you pass entry tests for a formal preparatory program but also can allow you to find out if you really are suited for the career.

There are also many Web sites that provide information about diving careers and marine science. Visit http://www.oceancareers. com for information about careers, training programs, and internships. Additionally, Sea Grant's Marine Careers Web site (http:// www.marinecareers.net) provides a general overview of marine science and career options in the field.

EMPLOYERS

The major employers of diving professionals are companies that search for petroleum and natural gas from undersea oil fields. Hydroelectric power generating plants, dams, heavy industry, and sanitation plants that have cooling water lines or water discharges are also a source of work for divers and surface crews. Certain ship repairs, usually of an emergency nature, require divers who can repair the trouble at sea or in dock, without placing the ship in dry dock to correct the problem.

While some work is being done in aquaculture, marine science, and ocean mining, these areas are currently relatively undeveloped. Although the potential for these fields is great and the possibilities for divers exciting, the total employment in these areas is presently small.

STARTING OUT

Commercial diving contractors, where the majority of diving professionals seek employment, have in the past recruited personnel from U.S. Navy training programs, informal apprenticeship programs, and through personal contacts. These employees had to learn on the job.

As diving technology advanced and diving equipment and techniques became more sophisticated, contractors looked more and more to schools to provide qualified entry-level help. Today, most commercial diving contractors primarily rely on approved schools to meet their entry-level personnel needs. Some contractors will hire only graduates of diving training programs.

Schools with diving technician programs usually have three or more staff members with professional commercial diving experience. These instructors keep abreast of the diving industry through occasional summer work, consultation, and professional and personal contacts. These contacts enable them to assess industry needs and to offer job placement help.

Major offshore contractors and other potential employers may visit schools with diving programs each year before graduation to interview prospective employees. Some employers offer summer work to students who have completed one year of a two-year program.

Some employers contact schools whenever they need additional diving personnel. The school staff then directs them to interested job seekers. While many graduates find jobs in oil-drilling operations or other large industries, a few graduates find positions as diving school instructors, aquaculture technicians, photographers/writers, marine research technicians, and submersible pilots.

You can also enter a diving career by joining the U.S. Navy or specialized units of the Marines, Army Corps of Engineers, or Merchant Marine Corps. Some U.S. military operations for salvage, recovery of sunken ships, or rescue require deepwater divers and life-support skills. Usually U.S. Navy and other experienced diving personnel can obtain civilian employment, but they often need to learn a wider range of skills for underwater construction or other work.

ADVANCEMENT

A well-trained, highly motivated diver or diving technician can expect to advance steadily, depending on personal competence and the employer's needs. Over a three- to five-year period a technician may be a shop hand, a *tender* (tending equipment and maintaining gear), a combination diver/tender, a diver, lead diver, and possibly supervisor of a diving crew. Or a technician may advance from surface support duties to supervisor of surface support or supervisor of a diving crew, possibly within three to five years. The nondiving life-support career, however, is much more limited in terms of employment opportunities than the combined diving and support career. Management opportunities within a company or research organization are also a possibility for qualified divers. Those who want greater opportunities for earnings, independence, and growth may start their own business as a contractor or consultant.

EARNINGS

Earnings in this career vary widely and depend on factors such as location, nature of the job, and the technician's skills or experience. A technician working in commercial diving might work almost anyplace in the oceans, rivers, and lakes of the world, although in the United States there is much work to be found in the Gulf of Mexico and in the Louisiana coastline, areas close to offshore wells. Some types of work, primarily union jobs, pay the employee on an hourly or daily basis. Diving professionals who work in marine research can also find opportunities throughout the world.

Recent graduates of diving technician programs often start in nondiving positions as tenders and earn around $10 to $11 an hour. An entry-level diver spends 200 days offshore and earns $100 take home pay per day on average, or between $20,000 and $24,000 a year. After several years of experience, a diver can earn $40,000 to $70,000 a year. The prevailing nonunion wage is about $33 to $41 an hour. The most experienced divers, who have at least 10 years of experience, can earn $60,000 to $100,000 a year.

The U.S. Department of Labor reports that commercial divers had median annual earnings of $52,540 in 2009. Salaries ranged from less than $32,510 to $94,130 or more.

Some contract jobs call for time on and time off, such as a 30 days on/30 days off rotation, and the pay will reflect at least a certain amount of the off-time as full-time pay. An example of a rotational job would be service work on an exploratory oil-drilling vessel where diving crew members live aboard for their on-shift period and perform any work required during that time. Wages earned under an organized union contract are typically higher, but the employee receives pay only for days worked. Because divers typically earn well, many divers choose to work only during the diving season, which takes place from June to December.

Employees of diving contractors typically receive life and health insurance benefits. Some companies also provide paid vacation time.

WORK ENVIRONMENT

Divers must possess numerous technical job skills. Working conditions may vary tremendously depending upon the nature of the work, the duration of the job, and the geographic location. Recreation specialists are frequently responsible for the welfare of inexperienced divers. Although they may work in a resort, under seemingly idyllic conditions, satisfying the needs of a group of diverse individuals may sometimes be stressful.

Some offshore sites include boats ranging from under 100 feet long to much longer oceangoing ships. Also, oil-drilling vessels, scientific research vessels, and many types of barges provide working and living bases for divers and diving technicians.

Working hours or shifts offshore may only require the diving crew to be available if needed, as is common on drilling vessels. More often, however, as in construction work, scientific research, or jobs that are continuous and predictable in nature, the dive crew will work up to 12 hours a day, seven days a week. As might be expected, the more rigorous work provides greater pay.

Living conditions aboard ship or barge are usually comfortable. Rooms may accommodate from two to as many as eight people, depending on vessel size. Food, of course, is furnished on all rigs where crews must live aboard.

Divers and diving technicians are taught to be conscious of appropriate clothing and safety practices and to follow these guidelines as they work in the potentially dangerous conditions encountered in deepwater diving.

Offshore work, especially construction diving, is rigorous and often physically demanding. Persons entering this field must be physically fit. Companies commonly place a maximum age limit, usually 30 to 32 years, for entry-level employees seeking to become divers. Although many divers work well into their 40s or 50s or older, long-duration deep diving is considered a young person's work.

Travel, excitement, and some amount of risk are a part of the diving professional's life. While on the job, divers and diving technicians should be self-starters, showing initiative and the ability to work independently as well as on a team.

People who choose a career in diving should be ready to adapt to a lifestyle that seldom offers stable home and family life. They must be able to follow the work and can expect occasional changes in job locations. There is also the reality of an uncertain work schedule, where a job might last for months or where the only available work may be on a short-term basis. Offshore work tends to run in a "feast or famine" pattern.

Divers and diving technicians must be confident of their own ability to cope with the uncertainties and risks of deepwater diving. They must be able to analyze and solve problems without panic or confusion. For most divers, there is real satisfaction in confidently and successfully performing tasks in an unconventional setting.

OUTLOOK

The U.S. Department of Labor reports that employment for commercial divers will grow more slowly than the average for all careers through 2018. Despite this prediction, there should continue to be good job opportunities for divers and diving technicians. The world is increasingly turning to the sea to supply mineral resources, new and additional sources of food and medicine, transportation, and national defense. There is also increasing demand for diving professionals to assist in ocean scientific research. This growth in marine activity has resulted in a continuing demand for qualified diving professionals. However, entry-level positions can be low paying and mostly on dry land, but with a few years of experience, gradually spending more time in the water and learning skills on the job, they usually are rewarded both in terms of pay and job satisfaction.

In the past few decades, the greatest demand for skilled diving professionals has been related to the search for more petroleum and natural gas from undersea oil fields. With the production of oil and gas from the oceans, there was a virtual explosion in the amount of work and the number of people employed. Whether this activity will be a source of new jobs in the future is uncertain. Employment will depend on levels of drilling activity, which, in turn, will depend on world oil prices. Traditionally, divers have been able to find jobs even during tough economic times, although it will take longer before a newcomer gets "wet" on an assignment.

FOR MORE INFORMATION

This organization for diving scientists stresses diving safety and offers internships for college students.
American Academy of Underwater Sciences
Dauphin Island Sea Lab
101 Bienville Boulevard
Dauphin Island, AL 36528-4603
Tel: 251-591-3775

E-mail: aaus@disl.org
http://www.aaus.org

For information on commercial diving and educational programs, contact the following organizations:
Association of Commercial Diving Educators
c/o Santa Barbara City College
721 Cliff Drive
Santa Barbara, CA 93109-2312
Tel: 805-965-0581, ext. 2426
E-mail: info@acde.us
http://www.acde.us

Association of Diving Contractors International
5206 FM 1960 West, Suite 202
Houston, TX 77069-4406
Tel: 281-893-8388
http://www.adc-int.org

For information on diving instruction and certification, contact these organizations.
NAUI Worldwide
PO Box 89789
Tampa, FL 33689-0413
Tel: 800-553-6284
E-mail: nauihq@naui.org
http://www.nauiww.org

Professional Association of Diving Instructors (PADI)
30151 Tomas Street
Rancho Santa Margarita, CA 92688-2125
Tel: 800-729-7234
http://www.padi.com

Geological Oceanographers

OVERVIEW

Oceanographers study the oceans of the world. *Geological oceanographers* are specialized oceanographers who study the topographic features, geological processes, and physical composition of the ocean bottom. Their work greatly contributes to our knowledge and understanding of Earth's geological history, as well as potential changes in the future, through observations, surveys, and experiments. Geological oceanographers are also known as *marine geologists.*

HISTORY

People have always been curious about the geological makeup of the oceans of the world, but serious scientific investigation did not occur until the 20th century because of the lack of technology that would allow scientists to conduct comprehensive research.

The origins of geological oceanography as we know it today can be traced to Project Mohole, an undersea drilling project that recovered the first sample of oceanic crust in 1961. In 1968, the U.S. National Science Foundation organized the Deep Sea Drilling Project (DSDP). The project collected core samples and rocks from the oceans of the world and helped scientists answer a wealth of questions about the geological composition of the ocean floor. Major discoveries included obtaining proof of seafloor renewal at rift zones and continental drift. In 1975, the DSDP was reconstituted as the International Program of Ocean Drilling (IPOD). Participating countries included the

A geological oceanographer holds a printout of a map of the Stellwagen Bank, an underwater plateau at the mouth of Massachusetts Bay. He used sophisticated sonar to map 1,400 square miles of ocean floor off the Massachusetts coast. *(Amelia Kunhardt, AP Photo/*The Patriot Ledger*)*

United States, France, the United Kingdom, Japan, the Soviet Union, and the Federal Republic of Germany. In 1985, the Ocean Drilling Program replaced IPOD. Major discoveries, according to the National Science Foundation, included "evidence of fluids circulating through the ridge flanks of the ocean floor, the formation of volcanoes and volcanic plateaus at rates unknown today, natural methane frozen deep within oceanic crust, and persistently rhythmic climate history." In 2003, the United States and Japan launched the Integrated Ocean Drilling Program (IODP). The IODP continues to study the ocean floor, and more discoveries can be expected in the future.

Drilling is not the only research method used by modern geological oceanographers. They also use satellites, sonar, remote-operated vehicles, and a variety of other technologies to explore, study, and map the ocean floor.

THE JOB

Geological oceanographers study the contour and materials of the seafloor (rocks, fossils, etc.) in order to draw conclusions about ocean circulation, climate, seafloor spreading, plate tectonics, and the ocean's geological features. They study physical features such as underwater mountains, rises and ridges, trenches, valleys, abyssal hills, and the ocean crust. They take sediment samples from the ocean floor to learn about the history of oceanic circulation and climates. Geological oceanographers study the physical and chemical properties of sediment samples, as well as their age, distribution, and origin—to learn more about historical and ongoing geological processes. They attempt to understand the origin of volcanoes and

Words to Learn

Abyssal plain: The deep ocean floor, an expanse of low relief at depths of 4,000 to 6,000 feet.

Aquarium: A place where living aquatic plants and animals are studied and exhibited. Also, a tank, bowl, or other water-filled structure in which living aquatic plants and animals are exhibited.

Conservation: The practice of preserving natural resources.

Coral reef: A living structure in the ocean that is made out of the exoskeletons of a tiny organism called a coral polyp.

Coriolis effect: The deflection of air or water bodies, relative to the solid earth beneath, as a result of the earth's eastward rotation.

Ecosystem: A group of organisms living together with nonliving components.

Ekman circulation: Movement of surface water at an angle from the wind as a result of the Coriolis effect.

Endangered species: A species having so few individual survivors that it may become extinct, or die off.

Epibenthic: Living on the surface of the bottom of the ocean.

Global warming: The slow rise in our planet's average temperature caused by an increase in greenhouse gases (such as carbon dioxide, methane, and nitrous oxide).

Tidal pool: A pool of seawater left on rocks near the ocean shore when the water (or tide) recedes. A variety of animals live in these temporary pools, including crabs, starfish, barnacles, small fish, and sea urchins.

Wetsuit: A garment that protects the wearer from the harsh conditions of the ocean or other bodies of water.

earthquakes and the gradual movement of the earth's surface. They also study erosional processes and the formation of hydrothermal vents.

Geological oceanography is considered to be one of the most diverse earth sciences fields, with many subspecialties. Some specializations include seismology, ocean drilling, ocean mining and oil and gas exploration, coastal geology, paleontology, geochronology, and petrology.

Seismologists use sound waves to study the earth's interior structure. They specialize in the study of earthquakes. With the aid of the seismogram and other instruments that record the location of earthquakes and the vibrations they cause, seismologists examine active fault lines and areas where earthquakes have occurred.

Geological oceanographers who specialize in ocean drilling collect soil and rock samples from beneath the ocean floor. One major international drilling project is the Integrated Ocean Drilling Program. According to Sea Grant, marine scientists participating in the program have made many major discoveries. They include "a new understanding of the causes and history of the ice ages, the evolution of the continental margins, [the] earth's tectonic processes, marine sedimentation, and the origin and evolution of the oceanic crust."

Those who specialize in ocean mining and oil and gas exploration search the ocean for potential sources of oil, gas, and minerals (such as manganese nodules that contain manganese, nickel, cobalt, copper; sand and gravel; phosphate; and other minerals).

Coastal geologists study the topographic features, geological processes, and physical composition of coastal regions. They also study effects of human development and nature on these regions.

Paleontologists specialize in the study of the earth's rock formations, including remains of plant and animal life, in order to understand the earth's evolution and estimate its age.

Geochronologists are geoscientists who use radioactive dating and other techniques to estimate the age of rock and other samples from an exploration site.

Petrologists study the origin and *composition* of igneous, metamorphic, and sedimentary rocks.

Geological oceanographers may spend some of their time on the water each year gathering data and making observations. They do additional oceanographic work on land. Experiments using mathematical modeling software or geological samples may be conducted in a seaside laboratory. They use Geographic Information Systems software to create 3-D computer maps of the seafloor. Geological oceanographers also collect data using satellites, seismic techniques, sonar, dredging processes, and, as mentioned earlier, deep-sea drilling projects.

Geological oceanographers usually work as part of a highly skilled, interdisciplinary team, often teaming with biological, chemical, and physical oceanographers and geologists, geophysicists, and other scientists and technicians on projects.

Some geological oceanographers teach at high schools and colleges and universities. Others write textbooks and articles about geological oceanography.

REQUIREMENTS

High School

To prepare for a career as a geological oceanographer, take a college preparatory curriculum that includes math classes, such as algebra, trigonometry, calculus, and statistics, and science courses, including chemistry, biology, and geology. Speech and English will help you hone your communication skills. Computer classes will come in handy since oceanographers use a variety of computer software and hardware to do their work. Taking a foreign language will be useful—especially if you plan to work abroad.

Postsecondary Training

Once in college, prospective geological oceanographers should continue to take science courses, including geology, biology, chemistry, and physics. While some universities do offer undergraduate oceanography programs, students who plan to go on to graduate school should not necessarily major in marine science or oceanography. In fact, most geological oceanographers concentrate on a related area of science, such as geology, chemistry, physics, or biology, before studying geological oceanography in graduate school. A well-rounded background in science is essential to a career as a geological oceanographer.

Students who plan to pursue an advanced degree in oceanography should look for institutions that offer significant hands-on research experience. More than 100 institutions offer programs in marine studies, and more than 35 universities offer graduate programs in oceanography.

Typical classes in a geological oceanography program include Introduction to Geological Oceanography, Marine Geological Processes, Marine Sedimentary Processes, Introduction to Sedimentary Geology, Marine Seismology, Geophysical Continuum Mechanics, and Physics of the Oceanic Lithosphere.

Many oceanography students participate in internships or work as teaching assistants while in college to gain hands on experience in the field. The American Society of Limnology and Oceanography offers a list of internships at its Web site, http://www.aslo.org.

Certification or Licensing
Oceanographers may scuba dive when conducting research. Organizations such as PADI provide basic certification (see For More Information for contact details).

Other Requirements
To succeed as a geological oceanographer, you must be intelligent, willing to work hard and at irregular hours, highly organized, and able to work closely with other people. Oceanographers must have superior computer and math skills. Cooperation is particularly important in this field, since oceanographers must work closely together on research projects. Because oceanographers must publish the results of their research, excellent writing skills are also essential. The most important characteristic for an oceanographer, however, may be intellectual curiosity. Oceanographers must yearn to solve nature's mysteries.

EXPLORING

Read books and visit Web sites about oceanography. One book suggestion is *Oceanography: An Invitation to Marine Science,* 7th ed., by Tom S. Garrison. Your school or community librarian can suggest many other resources. You can also visit Sea Grant's Marine Careers Web site (http://www.marinecareers.net) for information on careers, internships, volunteerships, and other activities, such as sea camps. Visit the Web sites of college oceanography departments, which offer information about the field, lists of typical classes, and details on internships. You may even be able to contact a professor or department head to ask a few questions about the career. Other ways to learn more about the field include asking your science teacher to arrange an information interview with a geological oceanographer and visiting an oceanography research center, such as Woods Hole Oceanographic Institution, or a local aquarium or even a zoo to learn about ocean environments.

EMPLOYERS

Approximately 23 percent of those working in oceanography and marine-related fields work for federal or state governments. Federal employers of geological oceanographers include the National Science Foundation, Departments of Commerce (National Oceanic and Atmospheric Administration), Defense, Energy, and Interior (National Park Service, Minerals Management Service); National Aeronautics and Space Administration; Environmental Protection Agency; Biological Resources Discipline of the U.S. Geological Survey, Naval Oceanographic Office, Naval Research Laboratory, and Office of Naval Research. State governments often employ oceanographers in environmental agencies or state-funded research projects.

Forty percent of oceanographers are employed by colleges or universities, where they teach, conduct research, write, and consult. The remaining oceanographers work for private industries such as oil and gas extraction companies and nonprofit organizations, including environmental societies.

STARTING OUT

Good sources of job leads for recent oceanography graduates include professors, contacts made during internships, and college career services offices. Additionally, the Marine Technology Society, American Society of Limnology and Oceanography, The Oceanography Society, and the Geological Society of America offer job listings at their Web sites.

ADVANCEMENT

Geological oceanographers advance by receiving higher salaries and by assuming administrative responsibilities. They also find work at larger organizations that are engaged in more prestigious research. The normal pattern of advancement for college professors is from instructor to assistant professor, to associate professor, to full professor.

EARNINGS

According to the U.S. Department of Labor, in 2009, salaries for geoscientists (an occupational group that includes geologists, geophysicists, and oceanographers) ranged from less than $43,140 to more than $161,260, with a median of $81,220. The average salary for experienced oceanographers working for the federal government was $105,671 in 2009.

Benefits for geological oceanographers depend on the employer; however, they usually include such items as health insurance, retirement or 401(k) plans, and paid vacation days. Oceanographers receive additional earnings from lecturing, consulting, and publishing their findings.

WORK ENVIRONMENT

Geological oceanographers work indoors in offices, laboratories, and classrooms and in outdoor settings such as the deck of a research vessel, a rocky beach, or in a submersible on the ocean floor. Those who conduct field research must be away from their families for long periods and live in close quarters with other marine scientists and support staff. Weather conditions vary greatly. On one expedition, a geological oceanographer may work in or near the icy water of the Arctic, and on another in the hot sun and balmy waters of tropical regions. Geological oceanographers who work as college professors spend only 12 to 16 hours a week in the actual classroom, but they spend many hours preparing lectures and lesson plans, grading papers and exams, and preparing grade reports. During holiday and summer breaks, they have the opportunity to travel and conduct research.

OUTLOOK

Employment for all geoscientists (including oceanographers) will grow faster than the average for all occupations through 2018, according to the U.S. Department of Labor. There is much yet to learn about the geological makeup of the ocean floor, which should translate into continued demand for geological oceanographers. Despite this prediction, competition for top positions will be strong. Those with a Ph.D., who speak a foreign language, and have a willingness to work abroad will have the best employment prospects.

As the nations of the world continue to search for new energy reserves and raw materials, opportunities for geological oceanographers who are employed by ocean mining and oil and gas exploration companies will be especially strong. Demand and supply, however, are difficult to predict and can change according to the world market situation; for example, the state of the offshore oil market can affect employment demand.

FOR MORE INFORMATION

For education and career information, contact the following organizations:

Acoustical Society of America
Two Huntington Quadrangle, Suite 1NO1
Melville, NY 11747-4502
Tel: 516-576-2360
E-mail: asa@aip.org
http://asa.aip.org

American Geophysical Union
2000 Florida Avenue, NW
Washington, DC 20009-1277
Tel: 800-966-2481
http://www.agu.org

This organization for diving scientists stresses diving safety and offers internships for college students.
American Academy of Underwater Sciences
Dauphin Island Sea Lab
101 Bienville Boulevard
Dauphin Island, AL 36528-4603
Tel: 251-591-3775
E-mail: aaus@disl.org
http://www.aaus.org

For information on careers in geology and chapters for college students, contact
American Association of Petroleum Geologists
PO Box 979
Tulsa, OK 74119-0979
Tel: 800-364-2274
http://www.aapg.org

For information on geoscience careers, contact
American Geological Institute
4220 King Street
Alexandria, VA 22302-1502
Tel: 703-379-2480
http://www.agiweb.org

For information on careers, contact
American Institute of Professional Geologists
12000 North Washington Street, Suite 285
Thornton, CO 80241-3134
Tel: 303-412-6205
http://www.aipg.org

Visit the society's Web site for information on careers and education.
American Society of Limnology and Oceanography
5400 Bosque Boulevard, Suite 680
Waco, TX 76710-4446
Tel: 800-929-2756

E-mail: business@aslo.org
http://www.aslo.org

For career information and profiles of women in geophysics, visit the association's Web site.
Association for Women Geoscientists
12000 North Washington Street, Suite 285
Thornton, CO 80241-3134
E-mail: office@awg.org
http://www.awg.org

For information on chapters for college students, contact
Association of Environmental and Engineering Geologists
PO Box 460518
Denver, CO 80246-0518
Tel: 303-757-2926
E-mail: aeg@aegweb.org
http://aegweb.org

For links to career information and sea programs, visit the following Web sites:
Careers in Oceanography, Marine Science, and Marine Biology
http://ocean.peterbrueggeman.com/career.html

Sea Grant Marine Careers
http://www.marinecareers.net

WomenOceanographers.org
http://www.womenoceanographers.org

For career information and job listings, contact
Geological Society of America
PO Box 9140
Boulder, CO 80301-9140
Tel: 888-443-4472
E-mail: gsaservice@geosociety.org
http://www.geosociety.org

For an overview of remote sensing, contact
Geoscience and Remote Sensing Society
Institute of Electrical and Electronics Engineers
445 Hoes Lane
Piscataway, NJ 08854-4141
E-mail: info@grss-ieee.org

http://www.grss-ieee.org

For information about careers, educational programs, scholarships, and student competitions, contact
Marine Technology Society
5565 Sterrett Place, Suite 108
Columbia, MD 21044-2606
Tel: 410-884-5330
http://www.mtsociety.org

For information on oceanography, contact
National Oceanic and Atmospheric Administration
U.S. Department of Commerce
1401 Constitution Avenue, NW, Room 5128
Washington, DC 20230-0001
http://www.noaa.gov

Contact the society for ocean news and information on membership.
The Oceanography Society
PO Box 1931
Rockville, MD 20849-1931
Tel: 301-251-7708
E-mail: info@tos.org
http://www.tos.org

For information on diving instruction and certification, contact
Professional Association of Diving Instructors (PADI)
30151 Tomas Street
Rancho Santa Margarita, CA 92688-2125
Tel: 800-729-7234
http://www.padi.com

For career information and job listings, contact
Seismological Society of America
201 Plaza Professional Building
El Cerrito, CA 94530-4003
Tel: 510-525-5474
E-mail: info@seismosoc.org
http://www.seismosoc.org

For information on careers in geophysics and student chapters at colleges and universities, contact
Society of Exploration Geophysicists
PO Box 702740

Tulsa, OK 74170-2740
Tel: 918-497-5500
http://www.seg.org

To learn more about coastal and marine geology, visit
U.S. Geological Survey: Coastal and Marine Geology Program
http://marine.usgs.gov

Laboratory Testing Technicians

OVERVIEW

Laboratory testing technicians who work in marine science conduct tests on countless substances such as seawater, rocks and minerals, and living organisms. Their laboratory duties include measuring and evaluating materials, recording data, and maintaining and ordering supplies.

HISTORY

The occupation of laboratory testing technician goes back almost to prehistoric times when humans first learned to convert earth-derived materials into tools, weapons, and medicines. Similarly, the early alchemists who experimented with various combinations of elements set the stage for the careers of the modern-day laboratory testing technician.

The career of laboratory testing technician really began with the onset of the industrial revolution. As production increased and technology became a large part of the new manufacturing processes, more and more laboratory technicians were hired to test products to make sure they met performance standards.

Today, laboratory testing technicians are employed in many fields, including oceanography.

QUICK FACTS

School Subjects
Chemistry
Earth science
Physics

Personal Skills
Following instructions
Technical/scientific

Work Environment
Primarily indoors
Primarily one location

Minimum Education Level
Some postsecondary training

Salary Range
$24,540 to $43,900 to $96,110+

Certification or Licensing
None available

Outlook
About as fast as the average

DOT
019, 022

GOE
02.05.01, 02.05.02

NOC
2212, 2221

O*NET-SOC
19-4021.00, 19-4031.00, 19-4041.00, 19-4091.00, 19-4099.00

THE JOB

Laboratory testing technicians help marine scientists study the world's oceans. They conduct tests on many substances. These may include seawater, sand, rocks and minerals, marine plants and animals, and biological samples (such as blood, tissue, and DNA) from marine life. Their tests help scientists answer a variety of questions and come up with strategies to protect the oceans. For example, a laboratory technician might conduct a test to determine how global climate change or pollution is affecting the world's oceans or if the cleanup of ocean waters and beaches after an oil spill was effective.

Regardless of the specific nature of the tests conducted by technicians, they must always keep detailed records of every step. Laboratory technicians often do a great deal of writing and must make charts, graphs, and other displays to illustrate results. They may be called on to interpret test results, to draw overall conclusions, and to make recommendations. Laboratory testing technicians must be comfortable using computer software programs such as Microsoft Word, Access, and Excel and computer graphic programs. Some technicians may have supervisory duties and manage small staffs of laboratory technicians.

REQUIREMENTS

High School
If working as a laboratory testing technician sounds interesting to you, you can prepare for this work by taking at least two years of mathematics and a year each of chemistry and physics in high school. You should also consider taking shop classes to become accustomed to working with tools and to develop manual dexterity. Classes in English and writing will provide you with good experience doing research and writing reports. Take computer classes so that you become familiar with using computer hardware and software. Other useful classes include earth science, biology, and marine science.

Postsecondary Training
A high school diploma is the minimum requirement for finding work as a laboratory testing technician. However, a two-year associate's degree in engineering, marine science, or marine biology—depending on the field you want to specialize in—is highly recommended and preferred by many employers. Completing the associate's degree will greatly enhance your resume, help you in finding full-time positions, and allow you to advance rapidly in your field.

Other Requirements
Laboratory technicians should be detail oriented and enjoy figuring out how things work. They should like problem solving and trouble-

shooting. Laboratory technicians must have the patience to repeat a test many times, perhaps even on the same substance. They must be able to follow directions carefully but also should be independent and motivated to work on their own until their assigned tasks are completed.

EXPLORING

Due to the precision and training required in the field, it is unlikely that as a high school student you will be able to find a part-time or summer job as a laboratory testing technician. However, you can explore the career by contacting local technical colleges and arranging to speak with a professor in the school's science technician program. Ask about the required classes, the opportunities available in your area, and any other questions you have. Through this connection you may also be able to contact a graduate of the program and arrange for an information interview with him or her. Although you probably won't be able to get work as a laboratory testing technician at this point, some research companies and plants do offer summer jobs to high school students to work in their offices or mail rooms. While these jobs do not offer hands-on technical experience, they do allow you to experience the work environment and make valuable contacts that might come in handy during your future job search.

EMPLOYERS

Laboratory technicians employed in marine science work for government agencies, colleges and universities, and for private industries such as oil and gas extraction companies and nonprofit organizations, including environmental societies. Federal government employers include the National Science Foundation; Departments of Commerce (National Oceanic and Atmospheric Administration), Defense, Energy, and Interior (Minerals Management Service); National Aeronautics and Space Administration; Environmental Protection Agency; Biological Resources Discipline of the U.S. Geological Survey; Naval Oceanographic Office; Naval Research Laboratory; and Office of Naval Research.

Outside of marine science, laboratory testing technicians work in almost every type of manufacturing industry that employs chemists or chemical engineers. They are needed wherever testing is carried on, whether it is for developing new products or improving current manufacturing procedures or for quality control purposes. They may assist biochemists, metallurgists, meteorologists, geologists, or other scientific personnel in large and small laboratories located all over the country. Many laboratory testing technicians work in the healthcare industry.

STARTING OUT

Technical schools often help place graduating technicians in jobs. Many government agencies and companies contact these schools directly looking for student employees or interns. Students can also contact local laboratories to find out about job openings in their area. Technicians often begin as trainees who are supervised by more experienced workers. As they gain experience, technicians take on more responsibilities and are allowed to work more independently.

ADVANCEMENT

Skilled laboratory technicians may be promoted to manager or supervisor of a division in their company or organization. Experienced technicians may start their own testing laboratories or return to school to become marine scientists, engineers, physicists, or geologists.

EARNINGS

Earnings for laboratory testing technicians vary based on the type of work they do, their education and experience, and even the size of the laboratory and its location. The U.S. Department of Labor reports the following mean annual earnings for science technicians (a category that includes laboratory testing technicians) in 2009 by specialty: biological technicians, $41,140; chemical technicians, $43,900; and geological and petroleum technicians, $58,400. Salaries for science technicians ranged from less than $24,540 to $96,110 or more.

Salaries increase as technicians gain experience and as they take on supervisory responsibility. Most organizations that employ laboratory testing technicians offer medical benefits, sick leave, and vacation time. However, these benefits will depend on the individual employer.

WORK ENVIRONMENT

Laboratory testing technicians typically work a 40-hour week. During especially busy times or in special circumstances, they may be required to work overtime. Most technicians work in clean, well-lighted laboratories where attention is paid to neatness and organization. Some laboratory testing technicians have their own offices, while others work in large single-room laboratories.

Some technicians may be required to go outside their laboratories to collect samples of materials for testing at locations that can be hot, cold, wet, muddy, and uncomfortable. Occasionally, laboratory testing technicians may be asked to participate in field research on ocean vessels. This will require them to be away from home for long periods of time and work closely—and efficiently—with an interdisciplinary team in close quarters.

OUTLOOK

Laboratory testing technicians who work in marine science should have good employment opportunities over the next decade. The oceans make up about 72 percent of the earth's surface, and scientists have yet to unlock all of the secrets hidden in their depths. Additionally, global climate change, increasing ocean pollution, and the mining and energy development of ocean resources will create demand for qualified technicians. Technicians in any specialty who have strong educational backgrounds, keep up with developing technologies, and demonstrate knowledge of testing equipment will have the best employment opportunities.

FOR MORE INFORMATION

The Education section of the institute's Web site has information on a number of careers in biology.
   American Institute of Biological Sciences
   1444 I Street, NW, Suite 200
   Washington, DC 20005-6535
   Tel: 202-628-1500
   http://www.aibs.org

Visit the society's Web site for information on careers and education.
   American Society of Limnology and Oceanography
   5400 Bosque Boulevard, Suite 680
   Waco, TX 76710-4446
   Tel: 800-929-2756
   E-mail: business@aslo.org
   http://www.aslo.org

For information on membership, a list of accredited zoos throughout the world, and careers in aquatic and marine science, including job listings, contact

Association of Zoos and Aquariums
8403 Colesville Road, Suite 710
Silver Spring, MD 20910-3314
Tel: 301-562-0777
http://www.aza.org

For information on member laboratories, visit the association's Web site.
National Association of Marine Laboratories
http://www.naml.org

Marine Biologists

OVERVIEW

Marine biologists study species of plants and animals living in saltwater, their interactions with one another, and how they influence and are influenced by environmental factors. Marine biology is a branch of the biological sciences, and biologists in this area work in myriad industries, including government agencies, universities, aquariums, and fish hatcheries, to name a few. They generally work either in a laboratory setting or in the field, which in this case means being in or on the ocean or its margins.

HISTORY

Marine biologists started to make their study into a real science around the 19th century with a series of British expeditions. In 1872, the HMS *Challenger* set sail with scientists Sir Charles Wyville Thomson and Sir John Murray on the most important oceanographic mission of all time. Over four years, they traveled 69,000 miles and cataloged 4,717 new species of marine plants and animals. Many marine scientists view the reports from this expedition as the basis of modern oceanography.

Before this time, marine scientists believed that sea creatures inhabited only shallow waters. They believed that the intense cold, pressure, and darkness below about 1,800 feet could not support life. Then, in the late 1860s, the HMS *Lightning* and the HMS *Porcupine* made hauls from below 14,400 feet that contained bizarre new creatures.

Scientists began to build precision equipment for measuring oceanic conditions. Among these were thermometers that could gauge the temperature at any depth, containers that could be closed at a

Books to Read

Kaplan, Eugene H. *Sensuous Seas: Tales of a Marine Biologist.* Princeton, N.J.: Princeton University Press, 2006.
Lear, Linda J. *Rachel Carson: Witness for Nature.* Boston, Mass.: Mariner Books, 2009.
Norse, Elliott A., and Larry B. Crowder. (eds.) *Marine Conservation Biology: The Science of Maintaining the Sea's Biodiversity.* Washington, D.C.: Island Press, 2005.
Stephens, Lester D., and Dale R. Calder. *Seafaring Scientist: Alfred Goldsborough Mayor, Pioneer in Marine Biology.* Columbia, S.C.: University of South Carolina Press, 2006.

desired depth to collect seawater, and coring instruments used to sample bottom sediments. Scientists also figured out techniques for measuring levels of salt, oxygen, and nutrients right on board ship.

Modern innovations such as underwater cameras, oxygen tanks, submersible craft, and heavy-duty diving gear that can withstand extremes of cold and pressure have made it possible for marine biologists to observe sea creatures in their natural habitats.

THE JOB

Marine biologists study and work with sea creatures in their natural environment, the oceans of the world and tidal pools along shore-lines, as well as in laboratories. These scientists are interested in knowing how the ocean's changing conditions, such as temperature and chemical pollutants, can affect the plants and animals that live there. For example, what happens when certain species become extinct or are no longer safe to be eaten? Marine biologists can begin to understand how the world's food supply is diminished and help come up with solutions that can change such problem situations.

The work of these scientists is also important for improving and controlling sport and commercial fishing. Through underwater exploration, marine biologists have discovered that humans are damaging the world's coral reefs. They have also charted the migration of whales and counted the decreasing numbers of certain species. They have observed dolphins being accidentally caught in tuna fishermen's nets. By writing reports and research papers about such discoveries, a marine biologist can inform others about problems that need attention and begin to make important changes that could help the world.

To study plants and animals, marine biologists spend some of their work time in the ocean wearing wetsuits to keep warm (because of the frigid temperature below the surface of the sea) and scuba gear to breathe underwater. They gather specimens with a slurp gun, which sucks fish into a specimen bag without injuring them. They must learn how to conduct their research without damaging the marine environment, which is delicate. Marine biologists must also face the threat to their own safety from dangerous fish and underwater conditions.

Marine biologists also study life in tidal pools along the shoreline. They might collect specimens at the same time of day for days at a time. They would keep samples from different pools separate and keep records of the pool's location and the types and measurements

A marine biologist at Padre Island National Seashore in Texas checks a green sea turtle for an electronic tracking tag. (*Michelle Christenson, AP Photo*/The Corpus Christi Caller-Times)

of the specimens taken. This ensures that the studies are as accurate as possible. After collecting specimens, they keep them in a portable aquarium tank on board ship. After returning to land, which may not be for weeks or months, marine biologists study specimens in a laboratory, often with other scientists working on the same study. They might, for example, check the amount of oxygen in a sea turtle's bloodstream to learn how the turtles can stay underwater for so long, or measure elements in the blood of an arctic fish to discover how it can survive frigid temperatures.

One growing subspecialty is marine biotechnology. *Marine biotechnologists* study ocean organisms that may be used for biotechnological applications, such as drug development or nontoxic coatings that repel fouling organisms such as zebra mussels on intake pipes in power plants.

REQUIREMENTS

High School

If you are interested in this career, begin your preparations by taking plenty of high school science classes, such as biology, chemistry, and earth science. Also take math classes and computer science classes, both of which will give you skills that you will use in doing research. In addition, take English classes, which will also help you develop research skills as well as writing skills. And, because you will probably need to extend your education beyond the level of a bachelor's degree, consider taking a foreign language. Many graduate programs require their students to meet a foreign language requirement.

Postsecondary Training

In college, take basic science courses such as biology, botany, and chemistry. However, your class choices don't end there. For instance, in biology you might be required to choose from marine invertebrate biology, ecology, oceanography, genetics, animal physiology, plant physiology, and aquatic plant biology. You might also be required to choose several more specific classes from such choices as ichthyology, vertebrate structure, population biology, developmental biology, biology of microorganisms, evolution, and cell biology. Classes in other subjects will also be required, such as computer science, math (including algebra, trigonometry, calculus, analytical geometry, and statistics), and physics.

Although it is possible to get a job as a marine biologist with just a bachelor's degree, such jobs likely will be low-paying technician positions with little advancement opportunities. Some positions in the field are available with a master's degree, but most marine biologists have a doctoral degree. Students at the graduate level begin to develop an area of specialization, such as *aquatic chemical ecology* (the study of chemicals and their effect on aquatic environments) and *bioinformatics* (the use of computer science, math, and statistics to analyze genetic information). Master's degree programs generally take two to three years to complete. Programs leading to a Ph.D. typically take four to five years to complete.

Certification or Licensing

If you are going to be diving, organizations like PADI provide basic certification. Training for scientific diving is more in-depth and requires passing an exam. It is also critical that divers learn cardiopulmonary resuscitation (CPR) and first aid. Also, if you'll be handling hazardous materials such as formaldehyde, strong acids, or radioactive nucleotides, you must be licensed.

Other Requirements

You should have an ability to ask questions and solve problems, observe small details carefully, do research, and analyze mathematical information. You should be inquisitive and must be able to think for yourself. This is essential to the scientific method. You must use your creative ability and be inventive in order to design experiments; these are the scientist's means of asking questions about the natural world. Working in the field often requires some strength and physical endurance, particularly if you are scuba diving or if you are doing fieldwork in tide pools, which can involve hiking over miles of shore at low tide, keeping your footing on slippery rocks, and lifting and turning stones to find specimens.

EXPLORING

Explore this career and your interest in it by joining your high school's science club. If the club is involved in any type of projects or experiments, you will have the opportunity to begin learning to work with others on a team as well as develop your science and lab skills. If you are lucky enough to live in a city with an aquarium, be sure to get either paid or volunteer work there. This is an excellent way to learn about marine life and about the life of a marine biologist. Visit Sea Grant's Marine Careers Web site (http://www.marinecareers.net) for links to information on internships, volunteerships, and other activities, such as sea camps.

You can begin diving training while you are in high school. If you are between the ages of 10 and 14, you can earn a junior open water diver certification from PADI. When you turn 15 you can upgrade your certification to open water diver.

EMPLOYERS

Employers in this field range from pharmaceutical companies researching marine sources for medicines to federal agencies that regulate marine fisheries, such as the National Oceanographic and Atmospheric Administration's National Marine Fisheries Service. Aquariums hire marine biologists to collect and study specimens.

After acquiring many years of experience, marine biologists with Ph.D.'s may be eligible for faculty positions at academic and research institutions such as the Scripps Institution of Oceanography or the University of Washington's School of Oceanography.

Marine products companies that manufacture carrageenan and agar (extracted from algae and used as thickening agents in foods) hire marine biologists to design and carry out research.

Jobs in marine biology are based mostly in coastal areas, though some biologists work inland as university professors or perhaps as *marine paleontologists* who search for and study marine fossils.

STARTING OUT

With a bachelor's degree only, you may be able to get a job as a laboratory technician in a state or federal agency. Some aquaria will hire you straight out of college, but generally it's easier to get a paid position if you have worked as a volunteer at an aquarium. You will need a more advanced degree to get into more technical positions such as consulting, writing for scientific journals, and conducting research.

Web sites are good resources for employment information. If you can find the human resources section of an aquarium's home page, it will tell you whom to contact to find out about openings and may even provide job listings. Federal agencies may also have Web sites with human resource information.

Professors who know you as a student might be able to help you locate a position through their contacts in the professional world.

Another good way to make contacts is by attending conferences or seminars sponsored by aquatic science organizations such as the American Society of Limnology and Oceanography or the Mid-Atlantic Marine Education Association.

ADVANCEMENT

Lab technicians with four-year degrees may advance to become senior lab techs after years with the same lab. Generally, though, taking on greater responsibility or getting into more technical work means having more education. Those wanting to do research (in any setting) will need a graduate degree or at least be working on one.

To get an administrative position with a marine products company or a faculty position at a university, marine biologists need at least a master's degree, and those wanting to become senior scientists at a marine station or full professors must have a doctoral degree.

EARNINGS

Salaries vary quite a lot depending on factors such as the person's level of education, the type of work (research, teaching, etc.), the size, location, and type of employer (for example, large university, government agency, or private company), and the person's level of work experience. According to the National Association of Colleges and Employers, those seeking their first job and holding bachelor's degrees in biological and life sciences had average salary offers of $33,254 in July 2009. The American Society of Limnology and Oceanography reports that those with bachelor's degrees may start out working for federal government agencies at the pay grades GS-5 to GS-7. In 2010 the yearly earnings at the GS-5 level ranged from $27,431 to $35,657, and yearly earnings at the GS-7 level ranged from $33,979 to $44,176.

College biological science teachers (including those who specialize in marine biology) had median annual salaries of $73,980 in 2009, according to the U.S. Department of Labor. Salaries ranged from less than $41,060 to more than $155,020.

All biological scientists, a classification that includes marine biologists, had annual earnings ranging from less than $44,990 to $138,820 or more, with a median of $82,390 in 2009, according to the U.S. Department of Labor. Marine biologists who hold top-ranking positions and have much experience, such as senior research scientists, may make more than these amounts.

Benefits vary by employer but often include such extras as health insurance and retirement plans.

WORK ENVIRONMENT

Most marine biologists don't actually spend a lot of time diving. However, researchers might spend a couple of hours periodically breathing from a scuba tank below some waters, like Monterey Bay or the Gulf of Maine. They might gather samples from the deck of a large research vessel during a two-month expedition, or they might meet with several other research biologists.

In most marine biology work, some portion of time is spent in the lab, analyzing samples of seawater or collating data on a computer. Many hours are spent in solitude, reading papers in scientific journals or writing papers for publication.

Instructors or professors work in classrooms interacting with students and directing student lab work.

Those who work for an aquarium, as consultants for private corporations, or in universities work an average of 40 to 50 hours a week.

OUTLOOK

There are more marine biologists than there are top positions at present. Changes in the earth's environment, such as global climate change and increased levels of heavy metals in the global water cycle, will most likely prompt more research and result in slightly more jobs in different subfields. Education is extremely important in this field. Most marine biologists in basic research positions have a Ph.D. Those with just a bachelor's or master's degree often work as science or engineering technicians, high school biology teachers, and in nonscientist positions related to biology such as marketing, sales, publishing, and research management.

Greater need for smart management of the world's fisheries, research by pharmaceutical companies into deriving medicines from marine organisms, and cultivation of marine food alternatives such as seaweeds and plankton are other factors that may increase the demand for marine biologists in the near future. Because of strong competition for jobs, however, employment should grow about as fast as the average for all careers.

FOR MORE INFORMATION

This organization for diving scientists stresses diving safety and offers internships for college students.

American Academy of Underwater Sciences
Dauphin Island Sea Lab
101 Bienville Boulevard
Dauphin Island, AL 36528-4603
Tel: 251-591-3775
E-mail: aaus@disl.org
http://www.aaus.org

For information on fisheries science, contact
American Fisheries Society
5410 Grosvenor Lane
Bethesda, MD 20814-2144
Tel: 301-897-8616
http://www.fisheries.org

The Education section of the institute's Web site has information on a number of careers in biology.

American Institute of Biological Sciences
1444 I Street, NW, Suite 200
Washington, DC 20005-6535
Tel: 202-628-1500
http://www.aibs.org

For information on careers, education, and publications, contact

American Society of Limnology and Oceanography
5400 Bosque Boulevard, Suite 680
Waco, TX 76710-4446
Tel: 800-929-2756
E-mail: business@aslo.org
http://www.aslo.org

For links to career information and sea programs, visit the following Web sites:

Careers in Oceanography, Marine Science, and Marine Biology
http://ocean.peterbrueggeman.com/career.html

Sea Grant Marine Careers
http://www.marinecareers.net

For reference lists, links to marine labs, summer intern and course opportunities, and links to career information, check out the following Web site:

Marine Biology Web
http://life.bio.sunysb.edu/marinebio/mbweb.html

Contact the society for ocean news and information on membership.

The Oceanography Society
PO Box 1931
Rockville, MD 20849-1931
Tel: 301-251-7708
E-mail: info@tos.org
http://www.tos.org

For information on diving instruction and certification, contact

Professional Association of Diving Instructors (PADI)
30151 Tomas Street
Rancho Santa Margarita, CA 92688-2125
Tel: 800-729-7234
http://www.padi.com

This center for research and education in global science currently runs more than 300 research programs and uses a fleet of four ships to conduct expeditions over the entire globe. For more information, contact

Scripps Institution of Oceanography
University of California–San Diego
8602 La Jolla Shores Drive
La Jolla, CA 92037-1508
Tel: 858-534-3624
http://www-sio.ucsd.edu

Marine Geophysicists

OVERVIEW

Geophysicists are concerned with matter and energy and how they interact. They study the physical properties and structure of the earth, from its interior to its upper atmosphere, including land surfaces, subsurfaces, and bodies of water. *Marine geophysicists* are specially trained geophysicists who study the oceans.

HISTORY

Geophysics is an important field that combines the sciences of geology and physics. Geology is the study of the history and composition of the earth as recorded by rock formations and fossils. Physics deals with all forms of energy, the properties of matter, and the relationship between energy and matter. The geophysicist is an "earth physicist," one who works with the physical aspects of the earth from its inner core to outer space.

This alliance between the earth and physical sciences is part of the progress that science has made in searching for new understandings of the world. Like the fields of biochemistry, biomathematics, space medicine, and nuclear physics, geophysics combines the knowledge of two disciplines. However, the importance of geophysics goes well beyond abstract theory. Marine geophysicists apply their knowledge to such practical problems as predicting earthquakes and tsunamis and locating raw materials and sources of power.

QUICK FACTS

School Subjects
Earth science
Physics

Personal Skills
Helping/teaching
Technical/scientific

Work Environment
Indoors and outdoors
One location with some travel

Minimum Education Level
Bachelor's degree

Salary Range
$43,140 to $81,220 to $161,260+

Certification or Licensing
None available

Outlook
Faster than the average

DOT
024

GOE
02.02.01

NOC
2113

O*NET-SOC
19-2021.00, 19-2012.00, 19-2042.00

THE JOB

Geophysicists use the principles and techniques of geology, physics, chemistry, mathematics, and engineering to perform tests and conduct research on the surface, atmosphere, waters, and solid bodies of the earth. They study seismic, gravitational, electrical, thermal, and magnetic phenomena to determine the structure and composition of the earth, as well as the forces causing movement and warping of the surface. *Marine geophysicists* are geophysicists who study the world's oceans. They conduct research on how matter and energy affect the ocean. In particular, they study the makeup of the earth's surface and waters and how geophysical phenomena such as earthquakes, tsunamis, and underwater volcanoes and hydrothermal systems change them.

Many geophysicists are involved in fieldwork, where they engage in exploration and prospecting. Others work in laboratories, where research activities are the main focus. They use mathematical modeling software to develop and test their hypotheses. Photogrammetry, Geographic Information Systems, and remote sensing technology is often used to gather geophysical data. In general, their instruments are highly complex and designed to take very precise measurements. Most marine geophysicists specialize in one of the following areas.

Applied geophysicists use data gathered from the air, ground, and ocean floor, as well as computers, to analyze the earth's crust. They look for oil and mineral deposits.

Exploration geophysicists, sometimes called *geophysical prospectors,* use seismic techniques to look for possible oil and gas deposits on land and beneath oceans. They may use sonar equipment to send sound waves deep into the earth or beneath the ocean surface. The resulting echo helps them estimate if an oil deposit lies hidden in the area.

Hydrologists study the physical and chemical properties of ocean waters. These include temperature, oxygen level, salt content, and amount of silicates, phosphates, and other chemicals that are present. They map and chart the flow and the disposition of sediments, measure changes in water volume, and collect data on the form and intensity of precipitation, as well as on the disposition of water through evaporation. Some hydrologists study glaciers and their sedimentation; others focus on studying acid rain.

Seismologists use sound waves to study the earth's interior structure. They specialize in the study of earthquakes. With the aid of the seismogram and other instruments that record the location of earthquakes and the vibrations they cause, seismologists examine active fault lines and areas where earthquakes have occurred. By studying the ocean floor, they can pinpoint areas where earthquakes may occur. Earthquakes can sometimes cause tsunamis, which can kill or injure people in regions far from the earthquake site. Seismologists also try to answer questions such as: What does the deep interior of the earth look like? and What is the role of upper earth mantle structures in tectonic plate interactions?

Tectonophysicists study the structure of mountains and ocean basins, the properties of the earth's crust, and the physical forces and processes that cause movements and changes in the structure of the earth. A great deal of their work is research, and their findings are helpful in locating oil and mineral deposits.

Volcanologists study volcanoes, their location, and their activity. They are concerned with their origins and the phenomena of their processes.

REQUIREMENTS

High School
A strong interest in the physical and earth sciences is essential for this field. You should take basic courses in earth science, physics, chemistry, and at least four years of mathematics. Advanced placement work in any of the mathematics and sciences is also helpful. Other recommended courses include mechanical drawing, shop, social studies, English, and computer science.

Postsecondary Training
A bachelor's degree in geophysics is required for most entry-level positions. Physics, mathematics, and chemistry majors can locate positions in geophysics, but some work in geology is highly desirable and often required, especially for certain government positions.

Graduate work at the master's or doctoral level is required for research, college teaching, and positions of a policy-making or policy-interpreting nature in private or government employment.

Many colleges and universities offer a bachelor's degree in geophysics, and a growing number of these institutions also award advanced degrees. An undergraduate major in geophysics is not usually required for entrance into a graduate program.

Some colleges offer degrees or specializations in marine geophysics. Typical classes include Biological Oceanography, Geological Oceanography, Chemical Oceanography, Physical Oceanography, General Chemistry, Earth Materials and Structure, Calculus, Marine Stratigraphy and Sedimentation, Marine Invertebrate Paleontology, Coastal Geology, Marine Geochemistry, Geographic Information Systems for Environmental Studies, and Remote Sensing Technology. Most students also complete at least one internship to gain hands-on experience and learn about potential career paths.

Other Requirements

Marine geophysicists should possess a strong aptitude in mathematics and science, particularly the physical and earth sciences, and an interest in observing nature, performing experiments, and studying the physical environment.

EXPLORING

You can explore various aspects of this field by taking earth and physical science courses. Units of study dealing with electricity, rocks and minerals, metals and metallurgy, the universe and space, and weather and climate may offer you an opportunity for further learning about the field. Hobbies that deal with radio, electronics, and rock or map collecting also offer opportunities to learn about the basic principles involved in geophysics.

Employment as an aide or helper with a geophysical field party may be available during the summer months and provide you with the opportunity to study the physical environment and interact with geophysicists.

To learn more about marine science and geophysics visit Sea Grant's Marine Careers Web site (http://www.marinecareers.net) for information on careers, internships, volunteerships, and other activities, such as sea camps. You can also read books about the field, visit the Web sites of college marine geophysics programs, and ask your science teacher to arrange an information interview with a marine geophysicist.

EMPLOYERS

Marine geophysicists are employed primarily by the petroleum industry, mining companies, exploration and consulting firms, and research institutions. A few geophysicists work as consultants, offering their services on a fee or contract basis. Many work for the federal government, mainly the National Geodetic Survey, the U.S. Geological Survey, and the Naval Oceanographic Office. Other geophysicists pursue teaching careers.

STARTING OUT

Most college career services offices are prepared to help students locate positions in business, industry, and government agencies.

Other job contacts can be made through professors, friends, and relatives. Some companies visit college campuses in the spring of each year to interview candidates who are interested in positions as geophysicists. College career services offices can usually provide helpful information on job opportunities in the field of geophysics.

Additionally, some associations—such as the American Geophysical Union, Geological Society of America, and the Seismological Society of America—offer job listings at their Web sites.

ADVANCEMENT

If employed by a private firm, a new employee with only a bachelor's degree will probably have an on-the-job training period. As a company trainee, the beginning geophysicist may be assigned to a number of different jobs. On a field party, the trainee will probably work with a junior geophysicist, which in many companies is the level of assignment received after the training has ended.

From a junior geophysicist, advancement is usually to intermediate geophysicist, and eventually to geophysicist. From this point, one can transfer to research positions or, if the geophysicist remains in fieldwork, to *party chief.*

The party chief coordinates the work of people in a crew, including trainees; junior, intermediate, and full geophysicists; surveyors; observers; drillers; shooters; and aides. Advancement with the company may eventually lead to supervisory and management positions.

Geophysicists can often transfer to other jobs in the fields of geology, physics, and engineering, depending on their qualifications and experience.

EARNINGS

The salaries of geophysicists are comparable to the earnings of those in other scientific professions. According to the U.S. Department of Labor, geoscientists (which include geologists, geophysicists, and oceanographers) earned an average salary of $81,220 in 2009. The lowest paid 10 percent earned less than $43,140 per year, while the highest paid 10 percent earned more than $161,260 annually. In 2009, the average salary for a geophysicist working for the federal government was $94,560. Both the federal government and private industry provide additional benefits, including vacations, retirement pensions, health and life insurance, and sick leave benefits.

Positions in colleges and universities offer annual salaries ranging from about $41,060 for instructors to $155,020 for full professors. Salaries depend upon experience, education, and professional rank.

Faculty members may teach in summer school for additional compensation and also engage in writing, consulting, and research for government, industry, or business.

Additional compensation is awarded to marine geophysicists who are required to live outside the United States.

WORK ENVIRONMENT

Marine geophysicists employed in laboratories or offices generally work a regular 40-hour week under typical office conditions. Field geophysicists work under a variety of conditions and often the hours are irregular. They are outdoors much of the time in all kinds of weather. The work requires carrying small tools and equipment and occasionally some heavy lifting. The field geophysicist is often required to travel and work in isolated areas or beneath the surface of the ocean in a submersible.

OUTLOOK

According to the *Occupational Outlook Handbook*, employment of all geophysicists is expected to grow faster than the average for all occupations through 2018. The total number of graduates with degrees in the geophysical sciences is expected to remain small and insufficient to meet the moderate increase in industry job openings. Those who specialize in marine geophysics should also have good opportunities. Marine geophysicists with advanced degrees, experience in the field, and a willingness to travel will have the best employment opportunities.

FOR MORE INFORMATION

For education and career information, contact
Acoustical Society of America
Two Huntington Quadrangle, Suite 1NO1
Melville, NY 11747-4502
Tel: 516-576-2360
E-mail: asa@aip.org
http://asa.aip.org

For information on careers in geology and student chapters, contact
American Association of Petroleum Geologists
PO Box 979
Tulsa, OK 74101-0979
Tel: 800-364-2274
http://www.aapg.org

For information on geoscience careers, contact
American Geological Institute
4220 King Street
Alexandria, VA 22302-1502
Tel: 703-379-2480
http://www.agiweb.org

For information on local meetings, publications, job opportunities, and science news, contact
American Geophysical Union
2000 Florida Avenue, NW
Washington, DC 20009-1277
Tel: 800-966-2481
http://www.agu.org

For information on careers, contact
American Institute of Professional Geologists
12000 North Washington Street, Suite 285
Thornton, CO 80241-3134
Tel: 303-412-6205
http://www.aipg.org

For career information and profiles of women in geophysics, visit the AWG Web site.
Association for Women Geoscientists (AWG)
12000 North Washington Street, Suite 285
Westminster, CO 80241-3134
Tel: 303-412-6219
E-mail: office@awg.org
http://www.awg.org

For information on college student chapters, contact
Association of Environmental and Engineering Geologists
PO Box 460518
Denver, CO 80246-0518
Tel: 303-757-2926
E-mail: aeg@aegweb.org
http://aegweb.org

For career information and job listings, contact
Geological Society of America
PO Box 9140
Boulder, CO 80301-9140
Tel: 888-443-4472

E-mail: gsaservice@geosociety.org
http://www.geosociety.org

For an overview of remote sensing, contact
Geoscience and Remote Sensing Society
Institute of Electrical and Electronics Engineers
445 Hoes Lane
Piscataway, NJ 08854-4141
E-mail: info@grss-ieee.org
http://www.grss-ieee.org

For information on marine geophysics and oceanography, contact
National Oceanic and Atmospheric Administration
U.S. Department of Commerce
1401 Constitution Avenue, NW, Room 5128
Washington, DC 20230-0001
http://www.noaa.gov

For career information and job listings, contact
Seismological Society of America
201 Plaza Professional Building
El Cerrito, CA 94530-4003
Tel: 510-525-5474
E-mail: info@seismosoc.org
http://www.seismosoc.org

*For information on careers in geophysics and student chapters at
colleges and universities, contact*
Society of Exploration Geophysicists
PO Box 702740
Tulsa, OK 74170-2740
Tel: 918-497-5500
http://www.seg.org

To read the online publication Become a Geophysicist . . . A What?,
visit
U.S. Geological Survey
http://earthquake.usgs.gov/learn/kids/become.php

To learn more about coastal and marine geology, visit
U.S. Geological Survey: Coastal and Marine Geology Program
http://marine.usgs.gov

Marine Mammal Trainers

OVERVIEW

Animal trainers teach animals to obey commands so that they can be counted on to perform these tasks in given situations. The animals can be trained for up to several hundred commands, to compete in shows or races, to perform tricks to entertain audiences, to protect property, or to act as guides for the disabled. *Marine mammal trainers* are animal trainers who work with dolphins, seals, whales, sea lions, walruses, and other marine mammals. Approximately 9,600 animal trainers are employed in the United States; only a small percentage of this group train marine mammals.

HISTORY

Animals have been used for their skills for hundreds of years. The St. Bernard has assisted in search and rescue missions in the Swiss Alps for more than 300 years. The German shepherd was used in Germany after the First World War to guide blind veterans.

The training of marine mammals as we know it today began in the 1960s and 1970s. As knowledge of animal behavior grew, trainers at zoos, aquariums and oceanariums, and amusement parks began to see the value of training marine mammals so that they could be cared for and managed more easily. An offshoot of this training was the animals' ability to "perform" for visitors who were eager to learn more about them.

In 1973, the International Marine Animal Trainers' Association was founded to represent the professional interests of marine mammal trainers.

THE JOB

Marine mammal trainers conduct programs consisting primarily of repetition and reward to teach animals to behave in a particular manner and to do it consistently. Each species of animal is trained by using the instincts and reward systems that are appropriate to that species. Sea mammals respond to both food and physical contact.

First, trainers evaluate an animal's temperament, ability, and aptitude to determine its trainability. Animals vary in personality, just as people do. Some animals are more stubborn, willful, or easily distracted and would not do well with rigid training programs. All animals can be trained at some level, but certain animals are more receptive to training.

By painstakingly repeating routines many times and rewarding the animal when it does what is expected, marine mammal trainers train an animal to obey or perform on command or, in certain situations, without command. In addition, marine mammal trainers are often responsible for the feeding, exercising, grooming, and general care of the animals, either handling the duties themselves or supervising other workers.

Trainers work with marine mammals for performance or for health reasons. For example, the dolphins and whales at the Shedd Aquarium in Chicago are trained to roll over, lift fins and tails, and open their mouths on command, so that much veterinary work can be done without anesthesia, which is always dangerous for animals. These skills are demonstrated for the public every day, so they function as a show for people, but the overriding reason for training the dolphins is to keep them healthy. Other training elements include teaching dolphins to retrieve items from the bottom of their pool, so that if any visitor throws or loses something in the pool, divers are not required to invade the dolphins' space.

Marine mammal trainers may participate in missions to rescue wild animals that are sick, injured, or stranded. If the animals can be rehabilitated, they can often be returned to the ocean.

Some marine mammal trainers are employed by the U.S. Navy. They train dolphins and sea lions to detect sea mines that can destroy U.S. ships and injure or kill U.S. military personnel.

REQUIREMENTS

High School

For high school students interested in becoming a marine mammal trainer, courses in anatomy, physiology, biology, and psychology will be helpful. Comprehending how the body and mind works helps

Trainers work with a beluga whale at a marine show in Bangkok, Thailand. *(Dinodia/The Image Works)*

a trainer understand the best methods for training. Knowledge of psychology will help the trainer recognize behaviors in the animals they train.

Postsecondary Training
Although there are no formal education requirements to enter this field, some positions do have educational requirements that include a college degree. Marine mammal trainers in circuses and the entertainment field may be required to have some education in animal psychology in addition to their caretaking experience. Zoo and aquarium animal trainers usually must have a bachelor's degree in a field related to animal management or animal physiology. Animal trainers who participate in rescue missions may require a background in veterinary medicine and care.

Moorpark College in Moorpark, California, offers an associate degree in exotic animal training and management. Visit its Web site, http://www.moorparkcollege.edu/departments/academic/exotic_ animal_training_and_management.shtml, for more information.

Most trainers begin their careers as keepers and gain on-the-job experience in evaluating the disposition, intelligence, and "trainability" of the animals they look after. At the same time, they learn to make friends with their charges, develop a rapport with them, and gain their confidence. The caretaking experience is an important building block in the education and success of a marine mammal trainer. Although previous training experience may give job applicants an advantage in being hired, they still will be expected to spend time caring for the animals before advancing to a trainer position.

Establishments that hire trainers often require previous animal-keeping experience, as proper care and feeding of animals is an essential part of a trainer's responsibilities. These positions serve as informal apprenticeships. The assistant may get to help a marine mammal trainer on certain tasks and will be able to watch and learn from other tasks being performed around him or her.

Certification or Licensing

Marine mammal trainers must have scuba certification. Organizations like PADI provide basic certification.

Other Requirements

Prospective marine mammal trainers should like and respect animals and have a genuine interest in working with them. Those who participate in shows and demonstrations for the public should have excellent communication and teaching skills. Trainers should also be in good physical condition and be able to lift up to 50 pounds when necessary. Other important skills are a strong work ethic and the ability to work well with others.

EXPLORING

Visit Web sites that provide information about marine mammals and careers in the field. One interesting Web site is DolphinTrainer.com. Created by marine mammal professionals, this site contains basic information on different careers and what it takes to enter the field. Visiting the Web sites of aquariums will also be useful.

You can also read books about the field. One suggestion is *Starting Your Career as a Marine Mammal Trainer*, 2nd ed., by Terry S. Samansky. It covers typical job duties, educational and training requirements, job-search techniques, and more. Ask your school or local librarian for some other suggestions.

Students wishing to enter this field would do well to learn as much as they can about marine mammals, especially animal psychology, either through course work or library study. Interviews with marine mammal trainers and tours of their workplaces might be arranged to provide firsthand information about the practical aspects of this occupation.

Volunteering offers an opportunity to begin training with marine mammals and learn firsthand about the tasks and routines involved in managing marine mammals, as well as train them. Part-time or volunteer work in animal shelters, pet-training programs, rescue centers, pet shops, or veterinary offices gives potential trainers a chance to discover whether they have the aptitude for working with animals in general. Introductory experience can be acquired, too, in summer jobs as animal caretakers at zoos, aquariums, amusement parks, and museums that feature live animal shows.

EMPLOYERS

Approximately 9,600 animal trainers are employed in the United States; only a small percentage of this group work as marine mammal trainers. The most common employers of marine mammal trainers are zoos, aquariums and oceanariums, amusement parks, and circuses. A few are employed by the U.S. military. Many are self-employed, and a few very successful marine mammal trainers work in the entertainment industry, training animal "actors" or working with wild and/or dangerous animals. A number of these positions require a great deal of traveling and even relocating. Although some new zoos and aquariums may open and others may expand their facilities, the number of job opportunities for marine mammal trainers at these facilities will remain relatively small.

STARTING OUT

People who wish to become marine mammal trainers generally start out as animal keepers, stable workers, or caretakers and rise to the position of trainer only after acquiring experience within the ranks of an organization. You can enter the field by applying directly for a job as an animal keeper, letting your employer or supervisor know of your ambition so you will eventually be considered for promotion. The same applies for volunteer positions. Learning as a volunteer is an excellent way to get hands-on experience, but you should be vocal in your interest in a paid position once you have gotten to know the staff and they have gotten to know you.

You should pay close attention to the training methods of any place at which you are considering working. No reputable organization, regardless of what it trains animals for, should use physical injury to train or discipline an animal. The techniques you learn at your first job determine the position you will qualify for after that.

You want to be sure that you are witnessing and learning from an organization that has a sound philosophy and training method for working with animals.

ADVANCEMENT

Most establishments have very small staffs of marine mammal trainers, which means that the opportunities for advancement are limited. The progression is from animal keeper to marine mammal trainer. A trainer who directs or supervises others may be designated head marine mammal trainer or senior marine mammal trainer.

Some marine mammal trainers go into business for themselves and, if successful, hire other trainers to work for them. Others become agents for animal acts. But promotion may mean moving from one organization to another and may require relocating to another city, depending on what animal you specialize in.

EARNINGS

Salaries of all animal trainers (including those who train marine mammals) can vary widely according to specialty and place of employment. Salaries ranged from less than $16,920 to $52,130 a year or more in 2009, according to the U.S. Department of Labor. The median salary for animal trainers was $26,930 in 2009. Those who earn higher salaries are in upper management and spend more time running the business or managing workers than working with animals.

Marine mammal trainers who work full time receive benefits such as vacation days, sick leave, health and life insurance, and a savings and pension program. Self-employed trainers must provide their own benefits.

WORK ENVIRONMENT

The working hours for marine mammal trainers vary considerably, depending on the type of animal, performance schedule, and whether travel is involved. When new animals are brought into zoos and aquariums, the hours can be long and quite irregular. Trainers may have to work at night and on weekends.

Marine mammal trainers work indoors and outdoors. In winter, trainers may work indoors, but depending on the animal, they may continue outdoor training year-round.

Marine mammal trainers work in the water and must feel comfortable in aquatic environments. Other aspects of the work may require bending or extended periods of standing or swimming.

Patience is essential in this job as well. Just as people do, animals have bad days where they won't work well and respond to commands. So even the best trainer encounters days of frustration where nothing seems to go well. Trainers must spend long hours repeating routines and rewarding their pupils for performing well, while never getting angry with them or punishing them when they fail to do what is expected. Calmness under stress is particularly important when dealing with wild animals.

OUTLOOK

Employment for animal care and service workers, which includes marine mammal trainers, is expected to grow much faster than the average for all careers though 2018, according to the U.S. Department of Labor. However, marine mammal training is a small profession, and many people want to enter the field, so competition for jobs will be keen. Applicants must be well qualified to overcome the heavy competition for available jobs. Some openings may be created as zoos and aquariums expand or provide more animal shows in an effort to increase revenue.

FOR MORE INFORMATION

Visit the alliance's Web site for information on marine mammals, internships, and publications.
  Alliance of Marine Mammal Parks and Aquariums
  E-mail: ammpa@aol.com
  http://www.ammpa.org

For information on membership, a list of accredited zoos throughout the world, and careers in aquatic and marine science, including job listings, contact
  Association of Zoos and Aquariums
  8403 Colesville Road, Suite 710
  Silver Spring, MD 20910-3314
  Tel: 301-562-0777
  http://www.aza.org

Visit the association's Web site for information on careers, endangered species, useful books and other publications, and student membership.
  International Marine Animal Trainers' Association
  1200 South Lake Shore Drive

Chicago, IL 60605-2490
Tel: 312-692-3193
E-mail: info@imata.org
http://www.imata.org

For information on diving instruction and certification, contact
Professional Association of Diving Instructors (PADI)
30151 Tomas Street
Rancho Santa Margarita, CA 92688-2125
Tel: 800-729-7234
http://www.padi.com

Marine Policy Experts and Lawyers

OVERVIEW

Marine policy experts are marine scientists who have extensive training in the social sciences, law, or business. They use this knowledge to help appointed and elected officials develop guidelines and policies for the wise use of ocean resources. *Lawyers,* or *attorneys*, provide legal representation for individuals, businesses, nonprofit organizations, and corporations. *Marine policy lawyers* are specialized attorneys who deal with a wide variety of ocean resource management issues such as policies and laws relating to states' and countries' legal rights to their nonliving and living ocean resources, coastal zone management, pollution, fishing rights, aquaculture, and marine archaeology.

HISTORY

In the United States, scientists and laypeople have advocated for the protection of ocean resources for more than 150 years. But it was not until the 20th century that people became serious about issues such as ocean pollution, overfishing, protecting endangered marine animals, and establishing marine reserves. Legal disputes that arise regarding the ownership of biological and physical resources (natural gas and oil deposits, etc.) in the oceans are another major marine policy issue. States and nations often negotiate, and sometimes go to court, to obtain the legal rights to these scientifically rich and financially lucrative areas. In the last 60 years or so, marine policy experts and lawyers have played a key role in advocating for the protection of ocean resources. They provide scientific and legal knowledge to politicians who are tasked with making important decisions about our oceans and coastal regions.

THE JOB

There are many policies and laws relating to coastal zone management, pollution, fishing rights, aquaculture, marine archaeology, and states' and countries' legal rights to nonliving and living ocean resources. If these laws and policies did not exist, people would have free rein to do whatever they wanted to the oceans, regardless of the negative effects their actions may have. For example, if there were no laws in place to protect marine fisheries, they might be so overfished that they would crash and may never recover (one example of such a crash occurred in the Georges Bank fishery off the coast of New England; laws were passed to ban fishing in the area and some fish stocks are very slowly rebounding). If people were allowed to dump trash or industrial waste from manufacturing processes into the ocean without any regulation, certain areas would quickly become so polluted that no life could exist or the fish harvested from these areas would be too unhealthy to eat. If countries did not respect the territorial rights of their neighbors, there would be more disputes relating to a variety of ocean issues—such as fishing rights, underwater archaeology, and sovereignty. Finally, if rare and endangered ecosystems, such as coral reefs, were not protected by national or international law, they could be destroyed and their diversity and beauty lost to humanity forever. Marine policy experts and lawyers help deal with these issues.

Marine policy experts are typically marine scientists with special training in business, law, the social sciences, and government. They work with elected and appointed officials to advocate for protection of the ocean and its resources. Many work for politicians in Washington, D.C., or in state capitals to advise them regarding marine policy. This work is fast-paced when legislative bodies are in session. Marine policy experts must prepare reports and talking points summarizing the issue at hand (for example, a dispute about fishing rights in ocean areas off the coast of Alaska or the pros and cons of creating a new marine reserve in U.S. waters in the Pacific). Marine policy experts spend much of their time meeting with people to convince them to support their boss's policy goals, while at the same time listening to the individual's or group's opinions regarding the issue. They meet with constituents, other congressional staff, and staff members of federal or state agencies that may be affected by the legislation.

Other marine policy experts work in the private sector for conservation and industry organizations and scientific societies. In conservation and industry organizations, marine policy experts follow legislation that is related to their group's goals (for example, fighting global warming, advocating against oil exploration off the coast of Florida, protecting fisheries in the North Atlantic, etc.). They work closely with politicians and their staffs to support or oppose legislation that is important to their organization. Marine policy experts who are employed by scientific organizations do not argue for or against legislation. Instead, they try to provide objective information to policy makers so that they can make informed decisions about the issue for their constituents. According to the American Society of Limnology and Oceanography, typical issues that a policy expert in this capacity might work on include "funding for scientific research (e.g., National Science Foundation), scientific ethics and guidelines, evolution in the classroom, and working with federal agencies to improve the quality of their science."

Some marine policy experts work as legislative affairs specialists for federal agencies, when they interact with Congress. They prepare agency officials for Congressional hearings and briefings by providing them with information about a particular marine policy issue. They also answer questions from members of Congress about these issues.

Marine policy experts may also work as *lobbyists,* who try to influence legislators to support legislation that favors certain causes or public interest groups.

Marine policy lawyers represent the interests of government agencies and private organizations concerning legal issues relating to ocean exploration, pollution, coastal zone management, fishing rights, and other matters. Their job is to help clients know their rights under the law and then help them achieve these rights before a judge, jury, government agency, or other legal forum. Some marine policy lawyers work with politicians to craft bills that will protect the environment. They may advise presidents and senators about the legal issues that are involved with creating new national parks, marine sanctuaries, or other protected areas.

Maritime lawyers, sometimes referred to as *admiralty lawyers,* specialize in laws regulating commerce and navigation on the high seas and any navigable waters, including inland lakes and rivers. Although there is a general maritime law, it operates in each country according to that country's courts, laws, and customs. Maritime law covers contracts, insurance, property damage, and personal injuries.

REQUIREMENTS

High School

If you would like to become a marine policy expert, take as many science and mathematics classes as possible in high school. Since you will frequently interact with constituents, politicians, and Congressional staffers, you should take English and speech classes to help you hone your communication skills. Other important classes include history, psychology, and computer science.

A high school diploma, a college degree, and three years of law school are minimum requirements for a law degree. A high school diploma is a first step on the ladder of education that a lawyer must climb. If you are considering a career in law, courses such as government, history, social studies, and economics provide a solid background for entering college-level courses. Speech courses are also helpful to build strong communication skills necessary for the profession. Also take advantage of any computer-related classes or experience you can get, because lawyers often use technology to research and interpret the law, from surfing the Internet to searching legal databases. Aspiring lawyers who plan to specialize in marine policy law should take as many science courses as possible.

Postsecondary Training

Marine policy experts typically have degrees in oceanography, marine science, ocean engineering, chemistry, biology, geology, or a related field. Some earn dual degrees in one of the aforementioned majors and business, political science, law, or communications. Most marine policy experts have a Ph.D. in a marine science-related field and many years of experience in their profession. Some marine scientists with a master's degree and considerable experience may be able to find a job in the field.

Many marine scientists break into marine policy careers by participating in Congressional fellowships. Those still in graduate school can apply to participate in the National Sea Grant (NSG) College Program Dean John A. Knauss Marine Policy Fellowship (http://www.nsgo.seagrant.org/Knauss.html). According to its Web site, the program "provides a unique educational experience to students who have an interest in ocean, coastal, and Great Lakes resources and in the national policy decisions affecting those resources...and matches highly qualified graduate students with 'hosts' in the legislative and executive branch of government located in the Washington, D.C. area, for a one-year paid fellowship." Those who have completed their Ph.D.'s can participate in the American Association for the Advancement of Science (AAAS) Science & Technology Policy Fellowships (http://fellowships.aaas.org). According to the organization's Web site, the fellowships "help to establish and nurture critical links between federal decision-makers and scientific professionals to support public policy that benefits the well-being of the nation and the planet."

To enter any law school approved by the American Bar Association, you must satisfactorily complete at least three, and usually four, years of college work. Most law schools do not specify any particular courses for prelaw education. A college student planning on specialization in marine policy law, however, might also take courses significantly related to that area, such as oceanography, marine science, or political science. Those interested should contact several law schools to learn more about any requirements and to see if they will accept credits from the college the student is planning to attend.

Currently, 200 law schools in the United States are approved by the American Bar Association; others, many of them night schools, are approved by state authorities only. Most of the approved law schools, however, do have night sessions to accommodate part-time students. Part-time courses of study usually take four years.

Law school training consists of required courses such as legal writing and research, contracts, criminal law, constitutional law, torts, and property. The second and third years may be devoted to specialized courses of interest to the student. The study of cases and decisions is of basic importance to the law student, who will be required to read and study thousands of these cases. A degree of juris doctor (J.D.) or bachelor of laws (LL.B.) is usually granted upon graduation. Some law students considering specialization, research, or teaching may go on for advanced study.

Most law schools require that applicants take the Law School Admission Test (LSAT), where prospective law students are tested on their critical thinking, writing, and reasoning abilities.

Certification or Licensing

Every state requires that lawyers be admitted to the bar of that state before they can practice. They require that applicants graduate from an approved law school and that they pass a written examination in the state in which they intend to practice. In a few states, graduates of law schools within the state are excused from these written examinations. After lawyers have been admitted to the bar in one state, they can practice in another state without taking a written examination if the states have reciprocity agreements; however, they will be required to meet certain state standards of good character and legal experience and pay any applicable fees.

Other Requirements

Marine policy experts should be very knowledgeable about their specialty (such as chemical oceanography, ocean engineering, or marine biology), have excellent communication skills, be able to work under deadline pressure, have good networking skills, and be able to multitask. They should be able to work at building coalitions and find common ground between opposing parties. They also must be ready to work long hours, including nights and weekends when legislative bodies are in session. Marine policy lawyers have to be effective communicators, work well with people, and be able to find creative solutions to problems, such as complex court cases. They should have a basic understanding of marine science and be passionate advocates regarding issues affecting our world's oceans.

EXPLORING

Learn as much as you can about marine policy issues, such as endangered species, ocean pollution, overfishing, and international land and resource disputes, by reading books and visiting Web sites. You can also visit Sea Grant's Marine Careers Web site (http://www.marinecareers.net) for information on careers, internships, volunteerships, and other activities, such as sea camps. These activities will provide you with an introduction to marine science. You can also ask a teacher or counselor to arrange an information interview with a marine policy expert about his or career. If you have trouble finding someone to interview, contact environmental organizations that deal with marine-related issues for potential interview leads.

If you think a career as a lawyer might be right up your alley, there are several ways you can find out more about it before making that final decision. First, sit in on a trial or two at your local or state courthouse. Try to focus mainly on the lawyer and take note of what he or she does. Write down questions you have and terms or actions you do not understand. Then, talk to your counselor and ask for help in setting up a telephone or in-person interview with a lawyer. Ask questions and get the scoop on what this career is really all about. Also, talk to your counselor or political science teacher about starting or joining a job-shadowing program. Job-shadowing programs allow you to follow a person in a certain career around for a day or two to get an idea of what goes on in a typical day. You may even be invited to help out with a few minor duties.

You can also search the Internet for general information about lawyers and current court cases. After you have done some research and talked to a lawyer and you still think you are destined for law school, try to get a part-time job in a law office. Ask your school counselor for help.

If you are already in law school, you might consider becoming a student member of the American Bar Association. Student members receive *Student Lawyer,* a magazine that contains useful information for aspiring lawyers. Sample articles from the magazine can be read at http://www.abanet.org/lsd/studentlawyer.

EMPLOYERS

Most marine policy experts are employed in Washington, D.C. Others work in state capitals that are located throughout the United States (but especially in states that border oceans). Policy experts work for legislatures, federal agencies that have an office of legislative affairs, conservation and industry organizations, and scientific societies. Marine policy lawyers work for government agencies and private organizations that deal with ocean-related issues. Some marine policy experts and lawyers are self-employed.

STARTING OUT

Marine policy experts typically enter the field after gaining experience as marine scientists. Many enter government positions after participating in NSG College Program Dean John A. Knauss Marine Policy Fellowships or AAAS Science & Technology Policy Fellowships. Those interested in working in the private sector should contact organizations directly for information on career opportunities.

The first steps in entering the law profession are graduation from an approved law school and passing a state bar examination. Usually, beginning lawyers do not go into solo practice right away. It is often difficult to become established, and additional experience is helpful to the beginning lawyer. Also, most lawyers do not specialize in a particular branch of law (such as marine policy law) without first gaining experience. Beginning lawyers usually work as assistants to experienced lawyers. At first they do mainly research and routine work. After a few years of successful experience, they may be ready to go out on their own. Other choices open to the beginning lawyer include joining an established law firm or entering into partnership with another lawyer. Positions are also available with banks, business corporations, insurance companies, private utilities, and with a number of government agencies at different levels.

Many new lawyers are recruited by law firms or other employers directly from law school. Recruiters come to the school and interview possible hires. Other new graduates can get job leads from local and state bar associations.

ADVANCEMENT

Marine policy experts advance by working for larger government agencies or organizations, or by working on more significant issues that are affecting oceans, such as global warming. They also may work as college professors, write books about marine science or marine policy law, or work as lobbyists.

Lawyers with outstanding ability can expect to go a long way in their profession. Novice lawyers generally start as law clerks, but as they prove themselves and develop their abilities, many opportunities for advancement will arise. They may be promoted to junior partner in a law firm or establish their own practice. Lawyers may enter politics and become judges, mayors, congressmen, or other government leaders. Top positions are available in business, too, for the qualified lawyer.

Marine policy experts and lawyers working for the federal government advance according to the civil service system.

EARNINGS

According to the U.S. Department of Labor (DOL), in 2009, salaries for geoscientists (an occupational group that includes geologists, geophysicists, and oceanographers) ranged from less than $43,140 to more than $161,260, with a median of $81,220. The average salary for experienced geoscientists working for the federal government was $91,030 in 2009.

In 2009, the median salary for practicing lawyers was $113,240, according to the DOL. Salaries ranged from less than $55,270 to $166,400 or more. Attorneys in the federal government earned mean annual salaries of $127,550. State and local government attorneys generally made less, earning $82,750 and $91,040, respectively.

Benefits include paid vacation, health, disability, life insurance, and retirement or pension plans.

WORK ENVIRONMENT

Offices and courtrooms are usually pleasant, although busy, places to work. Lawyers also spend significant amounts of time in law libraries conducting research. Many lawyers never work in a courtroom. Unless they are directly involved in litigation, they may never perform at a trial.

Marine policy experts and lawyers often have to work long hours, spending evenings and weekends preparing cases and research materials and interacting with politicians, Congressional aides, and others. Government marine policy experts may have to spend a considerable amount of time back in the home district of their bosses talking with constituents.

Both marine policy experts and lawyers may travel to coastal regions and other ocean sites to gather more information about a particular issue via hands-on research or by talking with marine scientists and local residents.

OUTLOOK

Employment for marine policy experts and lawyers should continue to be good through the next decade. The world's population continues to increase rapidly, and this places great stress (development, pollution, oil and gas exploration, etc.) on our oceans. Marine policy experts and lawyers will continue to play a key role in working with appointed and elected officials to develop wise policies for the study, use, and protection of ocean resources.

FOR MORE INFORMATION

For information about law student services offered by the ABA, contact
American Bar Association (ABA)
321 North Clark Street
Chicago, IL 60610-7598
Tel: 800-285-2221
E-mail: askaba@abanet.org
http://www.abanet.org

Visit the society's Web site for information on careers and education.
American Society of Limnology and Oceanography
5400 Bosque Boulevard, Suite 680
Waco, TX 76710-4446
Tel: 800-929-2756
E-mail: business@aslo.org
http://www.aslo.org

For information on workshops and seminars, contact
Association of American Law Schools
1201 Connecticut Avenue, NW, Suite 800
Washington, DC 20036-2717

Tel: 202-296-8851
E-mail: aals@aals.org
http://www.aals.org

The FBA provides information for lawyers and judges involved in federal practice.
Federal Bar Association (FBA)
1220 North Fillmore Street, Suite 444
Arlington, VA 22201-6501
Tel: 571-481-9100
E-mail: fba@fedbar.org
http://www.fedbar.org

For information on choosing a law school, law careers, and salaries, contact
National Association for Law Placement
1025 Connecticut Avenue, Suite 1110
Washington, DC 20036-5413
Tel: 202-835-1001
E-mail: info@nalp.org
http://www.nalp.org

For information on state courts, contact
National Center for State Courts
300 Newport Avenue
Williamsburg, VA 23185-4147
Tel: 800-616-6164
http://www.ncsconline.org

Contact the society for ocean news and information on membership for college students.
The Oceanography Society
PO Box 1931
Rockville, MD 20849-1931
Tel: 301-251-7708
E-mail: info@tos.org
http://www.tos.org

For industry information, contact
Society of Naval Architects and Marine Engineers
601 Pavonia Avenue
Jersey City, NJ 07306-2922
Tel: 800-798-2188
http://www.sname.org

Marine Services Technicians

OVERVIEW

Marine services technicians inspect, maintain, and repair marine vessels, from small boats, to specially built oceanographic research vessels, to large yachts. They work on vessels' hulls, engines, transmissions, navigational equipment, and electrical, propulsion, and refrigeration systems. Marine services technicians may work at boat dealerships, boat repair shops, boat engine manufacturers, or marinas. Others work in the field in support of scientific research expeditions or oil and gas exploration surveys. Naturally, jobs are concentrated near large bodies of water and coastal areas.

HISTORY

Ever since there have been boats and other water vessels, it has been necessary to have people who can repair and maintain them. In colonial times in the United States, those who took care of vessels were not called technicians, but they did many of the same routine tasks performed today, with less developed tools and equipment. Marine services technicians have had to keep up with developments in vessel design and material, from wood and iron to fiberglass.

QUICK FACTS

School Subjects
Mathematics
Technical/shop

Personal Skills
Following instructions
Mechanical/manipulative

Work Environment
Indoors and outdoors
One location with some
travel

Minimum Education Level
Some postsecondary training

Salary Range
$22,440 to $35,430 to
$55,030+

Certification or Licensing
Required for certain positions

Outlook
More slowly than the average

DOT
806

GOE
05.03.01

NOC
7335

O*NET-SOC
49-3051.00

THE JOB

Marine services technicians test and repair boat engines, transmissions, and propellers; rigging, masts, and sails; and navigational equipment and steering gear. They repair or replace defective parts and sometimes make new parts to meet special needs. They may also inspect and replace internal cabinets, refrigeration systems, electrical systems and equipment, sanitation facilities, hardware, and trim.

Marine services technicians who work for scientific research expeditions might repair boats ranging from small, two-person motorboats to massive research vessels that have specifically been built for long ocean voyages.

Workers with specialized skills often have more specific titles. For example, *motorboat mechanics* work on boat engines—those that are inboard, outboard, and inboard/outboard. Routine maintenance tasks include lubricating, cleaning, repairing, and adjusting parts.

Motorboat mechanics often use special testing equipment, such as engine analyzers, compression gauges, ammeters, and voltmeters, as well as other computerized diagnostic equipment. Technicians must know how to disassemble and reassemble components and refer to service manuals for directions and specifications. Motorboat workers often install and repair electronics, sanitation, and air-conditioning systems. They need a set of general and specialized tools, often provided by their employers; many mechanics gradually acquire their own tools, often spending up to thousands of dollars on this investment.

Marine electronics technicians work with vessels' electronic safety and navigational equipment, such as radar, depth sounders, loran (long-range navigation), autopilots, and compass systems. They install, repair, and calibrate equipment for proper functioning. Routine maintenance tasks include checking, cleaning, repairing, and replacing parts. Electronics technicians check for common causes of problems, such as loose connections and defective parts. They often rely on schematics and manufacturers' specification manuals to troubleshoot problems. These workers also must have a set of tools, including hand tools such as pliers, screwdrivers, and soldering irons. Other equipment, often supplied by their employers, includes voltmeters, ohmmeters, signal generators, ammeters, and oscilloscopes.

Technicians who are *field repairers* go to the vessel to do their work, perhaps at the marina dock. *Bench repairers,* on the other hand, work on equipment brought into shops.

Some technicians work only on vessel hulls. These are usually made of either wood or fiberglass. *Fiberglass repairers* work on fiberglass hulls, of which most pleasure crafts today are built. They reinforce damaged areas of the hull, grind damaged pieces with a sander, or cut them away with a jigsaw and replace them using resin-impregnated fiberglass cloth. They finish the repaired sections by sanding, painting with a gel-coat substance, and then buffing.

REQUIREMENTS

High School

Most employers prefer to hire applicants who have a high school diploma. If you are interested in this work, take mathematics classes and shop classes in metals, woodworking, and electronics while you are in high school. These classes will give you experience completing detailed and precise work. Shop classes will also give you experience using a variety of tools and reading blueprints. Take computer classes; you will probably be using this tool throughout your career for such things as diagnostic and design work. Science classes, such as physics, will also be beneficial to you. Finally, don't forget to take English classes. These classes will help you hone your reading and research skills, which will be needed when you consult technical manuals for repair and maintenance information throughout your career.

Postsecondary Training

Many marine services technicians learn their trade on the job. They find entry-level positions as general boatyard workers, doing such jobs as cleaning boat bottoms, and work their way into the position of service technician. Or they may be hired as trainees. They learn how to perform typical service tasks under the supervision of experienced mechanics and gradually complete more difficult work. The training period may last for about three years.

Other technicians decide to get more formal training and attend vocational or technical colleges for classes in engine repair, electronics, and fiberglass work. Some schools, such as Cape Fear Community College in North Carolina and Washington County Community College in Maine, have programs specifically for marine technicians (see For More Information). These schools often offer an associate's degree in areas such as applied science. Classes students take may include mathematics, physics, electricity, schematic reading, and circuit theory. Boat manufacturers and other types of institutions, such as the American Boatbuilders and Repairers Association, Mystic Seaport: The Museum of America and the Sea, and the WoodenBoat School, offer skills training through less formal courses and seminars that often last several days or a few weeks. The military services can also provide training in electronics.

Certification or Licensing

Those who test and repair marine radio transmitting equipment must have a general radio-telephone operator license from the Federal Communications Commission (445 12th Street, SW, Washington, DC 20554-0001, Tel: 888-225-5322, http://www.fcc.gov).

Certification for technicians in the marine electronics industry is voluntary, and is administered by the National Marine Electronics Association. There are three grades of certification for workers in this industry: the basic certified marine electronic technician (CMET) designation for technicians with one year of experience who pass the CMET examination with a score of 70 percent or higher, the advanced CMET designation for those with three years of experience who pass the advanced examination with a score of 70 percent or better, and the senior CMET designation for those with 10 years of experience who are approved by a majority vote of the certification committee.

Other Requirements

Most technicians work outdoors some of the time, and they are often required to test-drive the vessels they work on. This is considered an added benefit by many workers.

Technicians also need to be able to adapt to the cyclical nature of this business. They are often under a lot of pressure in the summer months, when most boat owners are enjoying the water and calling on technicians for service. On the other hand, they often have gaps in their work during the winter; some workers receive unemployment compensation at this time. Marine services technicians who are willing to travel around the world for work will have the best employment prospects, since there is always warm weather in some region of the planet.

Motorboat technicians' work can sometimes be physically demanding, requiring them to lift heavy outboard motors or other components. Electronics technicians, on the other hand, must be able to work with delicate parts, such as wires and circuit boards. They should have good eyesight, color vision, and good hearing (to listen for malfunctions revealed by sound).

Some marine services technicians may be required to provide their own hand tools. These tools are usually acquired over a period of time, but the collection may cost the mechanic hundreds if not thousands of dollars.

EXPLORING

This field lends itself to a lot of fun ways to explore job opportunities. Of course, having a boat of your own and working on it is one of the best means of preparation. If friends, neighbors, or relatives have boats, take trips with them and see how curious you are about what makes the vessel work. Offer to help do repairs to the boat, or at least watch while repairs are made and routine maintenance jobs are done. Clean up the deck, sand an old section of the hull, or polish the brass. If a boat just isn't available to you, try to find some type of engine to work on. Even working on an automobile engine will give you a taste of what this type of work is like.

Some high schools have co-op training programs through which students can look for positions with boat-related businesses, such as boat dealerships or even marinas. Check with your counselor about this possibility. You also can read trade magazines such as *Professional Mariner* (http://www.professionalmariner.com).

If you plan to work for an organization that conducts ocean research, it is a good idea to learn as much as you can about the field. Visit http://www.oceancareers.com for information about careers, training programs, and internships. Additionally, Sea Grant's Marine Careers Web site (http://www.marinecareers.net) provides a general overview of marine science and career options in the field.

EMPLOYERS

Marine services technicians are employed by scientific research organizations (government agencies, nonprofit environmental research organizations, etc.), oil and gas exploration companies, boat retailers, boat repair shops, boat engine manufacturers, boat rental firms, resorts, and marinas. The largest marinas are in coastal areas, such as Florida, New York, California, Texas, Massachusetts, and Louisiana; smaller ones are located near lakes and water recreation facilities such as campgrounds. Manufacturers of large fishing vessels also employ technicians for on-site mechanical support at fishing sites and competitive events.

STARTING OUT

A large percentage of technicians get their start by working as general boatyard laborers—cleaning boats, cutting grass, painting, and so on. After showing interest and ability, they can begin to work with experienced technicians and learn skills on the job. Some professional organizations, such as Marine Trades Association of New Jersey and Michigan Boating Industries Association, offer scholarships for those interested in marine technician training.

For those technicians who have attended vocational or technical colleges, career services offices of these schools may have information about job openings.

ADVANCEMENT

Many workers consider management and supervisory positions as job goals. After working for a number of years on actual repairs and maintenance, many technicians like to manage repair shops, supervise other workers, and deal with customers more directly. These positions require less physical labor but more communication and management skills. Many workers like to combine both aspects by becoming self-employed; they may have their own shops, attract their own jobs, and still get to do the technical work they enjoy.

Advancement often depends on an individual's interests. Some become marina managers, manufacturers' salespersons, or field representatives. Others take a different direction and work as boat brokers, selling boats. *Marine surveyors* verify the condition and value of boats; they are independent contractors hired by insurance companies and lending institutions such as banks.

EARNINGS

Motorboat mechanics had median annual earnings of $35,430 in 2009, according to the U.S. Department of Labor. Salaries ranged from less than $22,440 to more than $55,030 a year. Those employed in deep-sea, coastal, and Great Lakes water transportation had mean annual earnings of $44,900, those employed in inland water transportation had mean annual earnings of $42,360, and those working in ship and boat building earned $36,120 annually.

Technicians in small shops tend to receive few fringe benefits, but larger employers often offer paid vacations, sick leave, and health insurance. Some employers provide uniforms and tools and pay for work-related training.

WORK ENVIRONMENT

Technicians who work indoors often are in well-lit and ventilated shops. The work is cleaner than that on cars because there tends to be less grease and dirt on marine engines; instead, workers have to deal with water scum, heavy-duty paint, and fiberglass. In general, marine work is similar to other types of mechanical jobs, where workers encounter such things as noise when engines are being run and potential danger with power tools and chemicals. Also similar to other mechanics' work, sometimes technicians work alone on a job and at other times they work on a boat with other technicians. Unless a technician is self-employed, his or her work will likely be overseen by a supervisor of some kind. For any repair job, the technician may have to deal directly with customers.

Some mechanics, such as those who work at marinas or who work in the field, work primarily outdoors—and in all kinds of weather. In boats with no air-conditioning, the conditions in the summer can be hot and uncomfortable. Technicians often have to work in tight, uncomfortable places to perform repairs.

OUTLOOK

As boat design and construction become more complicated, the outlook will be best for technicians who complete formal training programs. Consolidations in the retail boat industry have impacted the demand for technicians, creating fewer jobs and limiting employment opportunities. The number of technicians who work for scientific research expeditions is small, but as more ocean research is conducted, there should continue to be opportunities for highly skilled technicians to keep research vessels in top condition.

FOR MORE INFORMATION

For industry information, contact
American Boatbuilders and Repairers Association
50 Water Street
Warren, RI 02885-3034
Tel: 401-247-0318
http://www.abbra.org

To learn more about oceanography, contact the following organizations:
American Society of Limnology and Oceanography
5400 Bosque Boulevard, Suite 680
Waco, TX 76710-4446
Tel: 800-929-2756
E-mail: business@aslo.org
http://www.aslo.org

National Oceanographic and Atmospheric Administration
1401 Constitution Avenue, NW, Room 5128
Washington, DC 20230-0001
http://www.careers.noaa.gov
http://www.noaa.gov

The Oceanography Society
PO Box 1931
Rockville, MD 20849-1931
Tel: 301-251-7708
E-mail: info@tos.org
http://www.tos.org

*To find out whether there is a marine association in your area,
contact*
Marine Retailers Association of America
PO Box 925
Boca Grande, FL 33921-0925
Tel: 941-964-2534
http://www.mraa.com

*For information on certification, the industry, and membership,
contact*
National Marine Electronics Association
7 Riggs Avenue
Severna Park, MD 21146-3819
Tel: 410-975-9425
E-mail: info@nmea.org
http://www.nmea.org

For educational information, contact the following schools:
Cape Fear Community College
411 North Front Street
Wilmington, NC 28401-3910
Tel: 910-362-7000
http://cfcc.edu

Washington County Community College
One College Drive
Calais, ME 04619-4046
Tel: 800-210-6932
E-mail: admissions@wccc.me.edu
http://www.wccc.me.edu

Marine Veterinarians

OVERVIEW

The *veterinarian*, or *doctor of veterinary medicine*, diagnoses and controls animal diseases, treats sick and injured animals medically and surgically, and prevents transmission of animal diseases. While most veterinarians treat pets and livestock, some specialized veterinarians care for marine animals such as dolphins, whales, fishes, and sea lions. They are known as *marine veterinarians*. This article will focus on these professionals. There are about 59,700 veterinarians in the United States. Only a small percentage specialize in treating marine animals.

HISTORY

The first school of veterinary medicine was opened in 1762 at Lyons, France. Nearly 100 years later, a French physician and veterinarian named Alexandre Francois Liautard immigrated to the United States and became a leader in the movement to establish veterinary medicine as a science. Through his efforts, an organization was started in 1863 that later became the American Veterinary Medical Association.

Veterinarians have been needed to care for marine animals ever since the first zoo and aquariums were founded, ocean rescue operations were undertaken to help injured or sick animals, and research was conducted to learn more about marine animals.

Marine veterinarians make up a small, but dedicated, specialty group in the larger field of veterinary science. They help zoos, aquariums, and other facilities that house and study marine life keep their animals healthy.

THE JOB

Veterinarians who care for marine life have many of the same responsibilities as traditional pet and livestock veterinarians. One of the main differences is that instead of caring for dogs, cats, horses,

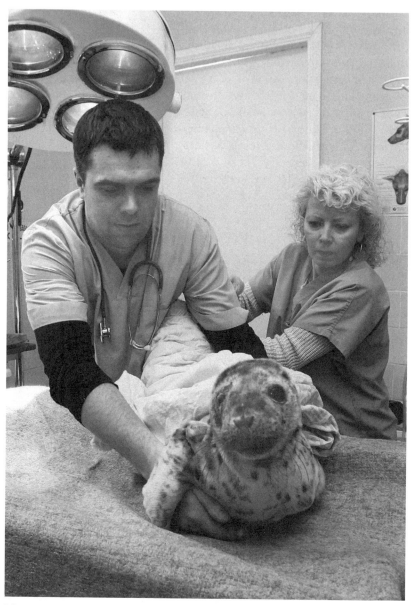

Marine veterinarians examine an injured seal pup found on the Baltic Sea coast near Kaliningrad, Russia. (*RIA Novosti/TopFoto/The Image Works*)

and cattle, they care for dolphins, whales, sea turtles, seals, otters, and other marine animals. Care of these animals may involve spending time in a water exhibit, working in a traditional office, or caring for animals in the ocean or on beaches.

Typical duties for veterinarians who work with marine animals include quarantining and observing new animals to ensure that they do not carry diseases; performing regular examinations, diagnosing illness or injury in animals, administering medication to ill or injured animals, prescribing rehabilitation regimens, setting fractures, treating and dressing wounds, performing surgery, helping to deliver offspring, and working with curators to develop animal diets, among other responsibilities. Additionally, veterinarians may have to euthanize (that is, humanely kill) an animal that is very sick or severely injured and cannot get well.

Veterinarians may also assist researchers with field projects, research and investigate diseases, rehabilitate wild animals, and serve as advocates for animals that are in captivity and in the wild throughout the world. Some veterinarians work as teachers at colleges and universities. Others write books and magazine articles about the field.

Veterinarians can become specialists in surgery, anesthesiology, dentistry, internal medicine, ophthalmology, or radiology. Many veterinarians also pursue advanced degrees in the basic sciences, such as anatomy, microbiology, and physiology.

REQUIREMENTS

High School
For the high school student who is interested in admission to a school of veterinary medicine, a college preparatory course is a wise choice. A strong emphasis on science classes such as biology, chemistry, and anatomy is highly recommended. Any experience working with marine animals is highly recommended.

Postsecondary Training
The doctor of veterinary medicine (D.V.M.) degree requires a minimum of four years of study at an accredited college of veterinary medicine. Although many of these colleges do not require a bachelor's degree for admission, most require applicants to have completed 45 to 90 hours of undergraduate study. It is possible to obtain preveterinary training at a junior college, but since admission to colleges of veterinary medicine is an extremely competitive process, most students receive degrees from four-year colleges before applying. In addition to academic instruction, veterinary education includes

clinical experience in diagnosing disease and treating animals, performing surgery, and performing laboratory work in anatomy, biochemistry, and other scientific and medical subjects.

There are 28 colleges of veterinary medicine in 26 states in the United States that are accredited by the Council on Education of the American Veterinary Medical Association (AVMA). Each college of veterinary medicine has its own preveterinary requirements, which typically include basic language arts, social sciences, humanities, mathematics, chemistry, and biological and physical sciences. Veterinarians can become specialists in surgery, anesthesiology, dentistry, internal medicine, ophthalmology, or radiology. Many veterinarians also pursue advanced degrees in the basic sciences, such as anatomy, microbiology, and physiology.

Applicants to schools of veterinary medicine usually must have grades of "B" or better, especially in the sciences. Applicants must take the Graduate Record Examination, the Veterinary College Admission Test, or the Medical College Admission Test. Only about one-third of applicants to schools of veterinary medicine are admitted, due to small class sizes and limited facilities. Most colleges give preference to candidates with animal- or veterinary-related experience. Colleges usually give preference to in-state applicants because most colleges of veterinary medicine are state supported. There are regional agreements in which states without veterinary schools send students to designated regional schools.

Veterinary medicine students typically participate in one or more internships during their college careers. The internships allow them to learn more about career options in the field and make valuable industry contacts. The American Association of Zoo Veterinarians, the International Association of Aquatic Animal Medicine, and the Alliance of Marine Mammal Parks and Aquariums offer information on internships at their Web sites.

Certification or Licensing

The American College of Zoological Medicine and the American College of Veterinary Behaviorists offer board certification to veterinarians who work with marine animals. Contact these organizations for more information. Specialty board certification is available in nearly 40 other specialty fields such as pathology, radiology, and surgery. Contact the AVMA American Board of Veterinary Specialties (http://www.avma.org/education/abvs) for more information.

All states and the District of Columbia require that veterinarians be licensed to practice private clinical medicine. To obtain a license, applicants must have a D.V.M. degree from an accredited or approved college of veterinary medicine. They must also pass one or more national examinations and an examination in the state in which they plan to practice.

Some states issue licenses without further examination to veterinarians already licensed by another state. Approximately half of the states require veterinarians to attend continuing education courses in order to maintain their licenses. Veterinarians may be employed by a government agency or at some academic institution without having a state license.

Other Requirements

Individuals who are interested in veterinary medicine should have an inquiring mind and keen powers of observation. Aptitude and interest in the biological sciences are important. Veterinarians need a lifelong interest in scientific learning as well as affection and understanding for animals. Veterinarians should be able to communicate and work well with many types of people.

Veterinarians use state-of-the-art medical equipment, such as electron microscopes, laser surgery, radiation therapy, and ultrasound, to diagnose animal diseases and to treat sick or injured animals. Although manual dexterity and physical stamina are often required, important roles in veterinary medicine can be adapted for those with disabilities.

EXPLORING

There are many ways to learn about a career as a marine veterinarian. One way is to read books about the field. Here are two suggestions: *The Rhino with Glue-On Shoes: And Other Surprising True Stories of Zoo Vets and Their Patients,* by Lucy H. Spelman and Ted Y. Mashima, and *Life at the Zoo: Behind the Scenes with the Animal Doctors,* by Phillip T. Robinson. You should also try to find part-time or volunteer work at zoos, aquariums, in small-animal clinics, or in pet shops, animal shelters, or research laboratories. Participation in extracurricular activities such as 4-H are good ways to learn about the care of animals (although 4-H will not give you an opportunity to work with marine animals). Such experience is important because, as already noted, many schools of veterinary medicine have established experience with animals as a criterion for admission to their programs. Finally, ask your science teacher to arrange an information interview with a marine veterinarian or a general veterinarian.

EMPLOYERS

Approximately 59,700 veterinarians are employed in the United States, with only a small percentage of this group working with marine animals. Marine veterinarians are employed by zoos, aquariums, wildlife management groups, research laboratories, and fish farms. They work for government agencies and in the private sector. Large facilities often have one or more veterinarians on staff, while smaller facilities contract with a veterinarian to provide care of their animals.

Veterinarians who do not specialize in treating marine animals have a variety of employment options. The vast majority work for veterinary clinical practices or hospitals. Others work for ranches, feed lots, pet food or pharmaceutical companies, and the government (mainly in the U.S. Departments of Agriculture, Health and Human Services, and Homeland Security).

STARTING OUT

The only way to become a veterinarian is through the prescribed degree program, and veterinary medicine schools are set up to assist their graduates in finding employment. Veterinarians who wish to enter private clinical practice must have a license to practice in their particular state before opening an office. Licenses are obtained by passing the state's examination.

Information about employment opportunities can be obtained by contacting employers directly or through career services offices of veterinary medicine colleges. Additionally, professional associations such as the American Association of Zoo Veterinarians, the American Association of Wildlife Veterinarians, the American Veterinary Medical Association, the Association of American Veterinary Medical Colleges, and the American Veterinary Medical Association offer job listings at their Web sites.

ADVANCEMENT

Veterinarians who are employed by zoos and aquariums advance by receiving pay raises, managerial responsibilities, or by finding employment at a more prestigious facility. Some very experienced veterinarians may become curators or directors of their facility. The veterinarian who is employed by a government agency may advance in grade and salary after accumulating time and experience on the job. For the veterinarian in private clinical practice, advancement usually consists of an expanding practice and the higher income that will result from it or becoming an owner of several practices. Those who teach or do research may obtain a doctorate and move from the rank of instructor to that of full professor, or they may advance to an administrative position.

EARNINGS

The U.S. Department of Labor reports that median annual earnings of veterinarians were $80,510 in 2009. Salaries ranged from less than $47,670 to more than $142,910. The mean annual salary for veterinarians working for the federal government was $84,200 in 2009.

Benefits include paid vacation, health, disability, life insurance, and retirement or pension plans.

WORK ENVIRONMENT

Marine veterinarians work in a variety of settings—from hospitals and operating rooms, to an animal's habitat in a zoo or aquarium, to the wild (animal rescue). They may work outdoors in all kinds of weather. The chief risk for veterinarians is injury by animals; however, modern tranquilizers and technology have made it much easier to work on all types of animals.

Most marine veterinarians work long hours. Those who are employed by zoos and aquariums are required to be on duty at night and on weekends.

OUTLOOK

Employment of veterinarians who treat pets and livestock is expected to be excellent through 2018, according to the U.S. Department of Labor. Opportunities will not be as strong for marine veterinarians. This specialty is very small, and many people want to work as marine veterinarians—especially at zoos and aquariums. Veterinarians with extensive experience working with marine animals will have the best employment prospects.

FOR MORE INFORMATION

Visit the alliance's Web site for information on marine mammals, internships, and publications.
Alliance of Marine Mammal Parks and Aquariums
E-mail: ammpa@aol.com
http://www.ammpa.org

Visit the association's Web site for job listings and information about wildlife veterinarians.
American Association of Wildlife Veterinarians

http://www.aawv.net*Visit the association's Web site for job listings, news about zoos around the world, the* Journal of Zoo & Wildlife Medicine, *information on internships and externships and zoo and wildlife clubs for veterinary students, and discussion boards.*
American Association of Zoo Veterinarians
581705 White Oak Road
Yulee, FL 32097-2169
Tel: 904-225-3275
http://www.aazv.org

For information on animal behavior, contact
American College of Veterinary Behaviorists
College of Veterinary Medicine, 4474 TAMU
Texas A&M University
College Stations, TX 77843-4474
http://www.dacvb.org

For information on certification, contact
American College of Zoological Medicine
Sacramento Zoological Society
3930 West Land Park Drive
Sacramento, CA 95822-1123
http://www.aczm.org

For more information on careers, schools, and resources, contact
American Veterinary Medical Association
1931 North Meacham Road, Suite 100
Schaumburg, IL 60173-4360
Tel: 800-248-2862
E-mail: avmainfo@avma.org
http://www.avma.org

For information on educational programs, contact
Association of American Veterinary Medical Colleges
1101 Vermont Avenue, NW, Suite 301
Washington, DC 20005-3539
Tel: 202-371-9195
http://www.aavmc.org

For information on membership, a list of accredited zoos through-out the world, and careers in aquatic and marine science, including job listings, contact

Association of Zoos and Aquariums
8403 Colesville Road, Suite 710
Silver Spring, MD 20910-3314
Tel: 301-562-0777
http://www.aza.org

For information on education and internships, contact

International Association of Aquatic Animal Medicine
E-mail: fmb@resoundinternational.org.uk
http://www.iaaam.org

For information about educational programs and workshops, and to read article about industry-related news, visit the following Web site:

Marine Veterinary Medicine
PO Box 882
College Station, TX 77841-0882
Tel: 979-764-9193
E-mail: info@marvet.org
http://www.marvet.org/

Ocean Engineers

OVERVIEW

Engineers are problem-solvers who use the principles of mathematics and science to plan, design, and create ways to make things work better. *Ocean engineers* use their scientific and technical knowledge to design and build instruments, tools, and machinery that assist oceanographers and other marine scientists in their research. They are also called *oceanographic* and *coastal engineers*.

HISTORY

Engineers have influenced discoveries and inventions more than workers in any other profession. The work of engineers has a more thorough impact on all human life than any other discipline.

Ocean engineers play a very important role in the field of marine science. In fact, many credit ocean engineers with revolutionizing the field of oceanography. The equipment, instruments, and tools that ocean engineers have designed and built have allowed marine scientists to journey deeper into the ocean depths, gather a larger amount of research, and keep scientists safe as they conduct their studies. According to the National Oceanic and Atmospheric Administration, major oceanographic discoveries—such as ocean volcanoes, hydrothermal vents, and "new" species—would not have been made without the help of ocean engineers.

THE JOB

The individuals who specialize in designing and building equipment, instruments, and tools for ocean research are called *ocean engineers.* Examples of these objects include underwater high-definition video cameras, acoustic measuring devices, underwater vehicles (such as submersibles and remotely operated vehicles), computer- and satellite-linked floats and buoys, offshore aquaculture cages, sediment traps, ocean seismometers (an instrument that measures earth move-

QUICK FACTS

(continued)

17-2072.00, 17-2081.00, 17-2121.01, 17-2121.02, 17-2131.00, 17-2141.00, 17-2151.00, 17-2161.00, 17-2171.00, 17-2199.99

ment on the seafloor), programmable buoys, and portable lighting systems that work in the ocean depths.

Ocean engineering is actually an interdisciplinary combination of many engineering specialties (including acoustical, chemical, civil, electrical, electronics, hardware, marine, materials, mechanical, and software engineering) and marine science principles, physics, and mathematics.

To design oceanography instruments, ocean engineers must understand research methods and the way materials react to conditions beneath the ocean's surface. The lives of marine scientists, as well as their ability to gather accurate research, are at stake. For example, great pressure exists in the depths of the ocean, and equipment must continue to work and not be damaged when used deep below the surface. Salt water is another enemy of ocean engineers. Because it is highly corrosive, engineers must carefully consider the materials that will be used when designing high-performance tools and equipment. Oceanographic research equipment must also be built to withstand the elements—such as high wind, rough waves, storms, extremes in cold and heat, and strong currents—as well as fouling by marine life such as barnacles and zebra mussels.

Coastal engineering is a subdiscipline of ocean engineering. *Coastal engineers* deal with erosion, pollution, and waste disposal issues on coastlines.

Naval and marine engineers work with *naval architects* to design the most efficient and cost-effective military and commercial passenger and cargo vessels, submersibles, and submarines. Their skills are also in demand by energy companies involved in underwater exploration. Some engineering professionals consider naval and marine engineering a subdiscipline of ocean engineering, others view it is a distinct engineering field.

Ocean engineers engage in one of five areas of study: The first stage of any project is research. Ocean engineers who work in research are responsible for investigating new materials, processes, or principles for practical applications of ideas and materials. For example, a research engineer might research the properties and principals of a new tool or piece of equipment.

Development follows research. Engineers working in the area of development take the results of the research and begin thinking about how best to apply them to their practical functions. A *development engineer* might develop a plan for using properties of radar in tracking weather systems.

Application is the actual production of an idea developed. Engineers take the product from development and establish ways of designing and producing the materials, machines, methods, or other results of research and development. It is at this stage that the concepts become usable to the people outside of engineering. Taking the radar example, a new radar device for tracking and monitoring hurricanes may be created in applied engineering. It isn't until this stage that the research and development areas affect the average person. However, the applications area would not exist if it weren't for the other two.

Management and maintenance are the final stages of engineering work. These engineers are responsible for keeping the developed idea working. Without some form of upkeep and improvement, engineering discoveries would be lost.

Project engineers are in charge of entire engineering projects. They schedule and oversee every stage of a project, ensuring that each stage is completed in an efficient and timely fashion. They must make sure that the project is completed according to standard procedures and regulations.

Ocean engineers are assisted by ocean engineering technicians and technologists. These workers are differentiated most commonly by the type of education they receive. Engineering technicians typically have an associate degree in engineering technology, although some learn their skills via a combination of postsecondary training and on-the-job training. Engineering technologists typically have a bachelor's degree in engineering technology. Some engineering technicians and technologists go back to school to become engineers.

REQUIREMENTS

High School

High school students who are interested in ocean engineering should take a great deal of mathematics, including geometry, trigonometry, calculus, and two years of algebra. They should develop a strong background in science by taking classes in physics, chemistry, biology, as well as taking course work in computer programming, computer-aided design, or applications. Because engineers must communicate constantly with other engineers, scientists, clients, and consumers, four years of language arts are essential.

Postsecondary Training

Many ocean engineers earn a bachelor's degree in another engineering specialty, such as mechanical, civil, or electrical engineering, before earning a master's degree in ocean engineering. Others pursue bachelor's degrees in oceanography, marine science, marine technology, or related fields.

The Accreditation Board for Engineering and Technology (ABET) accredits postsecondary ocean engineering programs. Currently there are only eight ocean engineering programs accredited by ABET. Visit its Web site for a complete list. Typical ocean engineering classes include Introduction to Ocean Engineering, Ocean Instrumentation, Ocean Engineering Design Tools, Ocean Engineering Design, Fundamentals of Ocean Mechanics, Basic Ocean Measurement, Introduction to Engineering Wave Mechanics, Marine Structure Design, Underwater Acoustics, Sonar Systems Design, and Corrosion and Corrosion Control.

Certification or Licensing

Many engineers become certified. Certification is a status granted by a technical or professional organization for the purpose of recognizing and documenting an individual's abilities in a specific engineering field.

Licensure as a professional engineer is recommended since an increasing number of employers require it. Even those employers who do not require licensing will view it favorably when considering new hires or when reviewing workers for promotion. Licensing requirements vary from state to state. In general, however, they involve having graduated from an accredited school, having four years of work experience, and having passed the eight-hour Fundamentals of Engineering exam and the eight-hour Principles and Practice of Engineering exam. Depending on your state, you can take the Fundamentals exam shortly before your graduation from college or after you have received your bachelor's degree. At that point you will be an engineer-in-training (EIT). Once you have fulfilled all the licensure requirements, you receive the designation professional engineer (PE). Visit the NCEES Web site, http://www.ncees.org, for more information on licensure.

Other Requirements

Students who are interested in becoming ocean engineers should enjoy solving problems, developing logical plans, and designing things. They should have a strong interest and ability in science and mathematics and enjoy creating tools, equipment, and instrumentation for ocean environments. Engineers often work on projects in teams, so prospective engineers should be able to work well both alone and with others.

EXPLORING

Perhaps the best way for high school students to explore the general field of engineering is by contacting the Junior Engineering Technical Society (JETS). JETS can help students learn about different fields within engineering and can guide students toward science and engineering fairs.

Participation in science and engineering fairs can be an invaluable experience for a high school student interested in engineering. Through these fairs, students learn to do their own research and applications in an engineering field. Too often, students leave high school with a strong academic background in mathematics and sciences, but have never applied their knowledge to the real world. By developing a project for a fair, students begin to learn how to think like an engineer by creatively using their academic knowledge to solve real-life problems.

The Marine Technology Society offers competitions, internships, workshops, and institutes that allow high school students to explore careers in ocean engineering. Visit its Web site, http://www.mtsociety.org, for more information.

You can also learn more about ocean engineering by talking to ocean engineers about their careers and visiting Web sites about the field. Two Web site suggestions are Sea Grant Marine Careers (http://www.marinecareers.net) and eGFI: Dream Up the Future: Ocean Engineering (http://www.egfi-k12.org/#/cards/ocean).

EMPLOYERS

Ocean engineers are employed by government agencies that study oceans and the environment, the U.S. military, private industry, defense contractors, oil and gas exploration companies, marine archaeology firms, consulting firms, and any other organization that conducts ocean research. Other possibilities for ocean engineers can be found in academia as instructors or researchers or as writers for engineering-oriented publications.

STARTING OUT

College and graduate school programs can help newly degreed ocean engineers locate jobs. These schools are often in touch with prospective employers who are in need of engineers. College ocean engineering departments may also maintain lists of employers of recent graduates. Conferences, trade shows, and engineering career fairs can also be good places for new engineers to begin meeting employers and setting up interviews

ADVANCEMENT

As ocean engineers gain more experience, they are given greater responsibilities and tougher problems to solve. At this stage, the engineer will be involved in more decision making and independent work. Some ocean engineers advance to become engineering team managers or supervisors of entire projects. They also may enter administrative or sales positions. In addition, many high-level corporate and government executives started out as engineers.

Advancement depends upon experience and education. The more experience ocean engineers get, the more independence and responsibilities they will probably gain; however, an engineer with a bachelor's degree will, in all probability, not make it to the highest levels of the field. Ocean engineers who are interested in going into corporate, industrial, or executive positions often go back to school to earn degrees in law or business.

EARNINGS

Engineers earn some of the highest starting salaries of any career. In 2009, the National Association of Colleges and Employers reported that engineers with a bachelor's degree earned the following starting salaries by specialty: chemical, $64,902; civil, $52,048; computer, $61,738; electrical/electronics and communications, $60,125; mechanical, $58,766; and materials, $57,349. In 2009, mean annual salaries for all engineers ranged from less than $79,240 (marine engineers) to $101,410 (computer hardware engineers) or more, according to the U.S. Department of Labor. Median annual salaries for all engineers working for the federal government ranged from $81,085 to $126,788 in 2009.

Ocean engineers who work for a company or government agency usually receive benefits such as vacation days, sick leave, health and life insurance, and a savings and pension program. Self-employed engineers must provide their own benefits.

WORK ENVIRONMENT

Ocean engineers usually have a central office from which they base their work, and these offices are typically quite pleasant, clean, and climate controlled. Engineers often have clerical, research, and technical staffs working for them at these offices.

Most ocean engineers, however, spend a considerable amount of time in the field testing and troubleshooting their designs and discussing the engineering process with marine scientists. They work outside in all weather conditions and spend time at sea as necessary. People interested in becoming ocean engineers should be flexible about work sites and adjust easily to different types of environments.

OUTLOOK

Employment for all engineers is expected to grow about as fast as the average for all occupations through 2018, according to the U.S. Department of Labor. Job opportunities for ocean engineers should also be good. There are many areas of our world's oceans that are unexplored, and since technology plays such an important role in this exploration and research, ocean engineers will continue to be in demand. As development continues on our nation's coastlines, there will also be a need for ocean engineers to help address problems with erosion, pollution, and waste disposal.

FOR MORE INFORMATION

For a list of accredited schools and colleges, contact
Accreditation Board for Engineering and Technology Inc.
111 Market Place, Suite 1050
Baltimore, MD 21202-7116
Tel: 410-347-7700
http://www.abet.org

For education and career information, contact
Acoustical Society of America
Two Huntington Quadrangle, Suite 1NO1
Melville, NY 11747-4502
Tel: 516-576-2360
E-mail: asa@aip.org
http://asa.aip.org

For information on engineering specialty associations, contact
American Association of Engineering Societies
6522 Meadowridge Road Suite 101
Elkridge, MD 21075-6191
Tel: 202-296-2237
http://www.aaes.org

For more information about careers in engineering, contact
American Society for Engineering Education
1818 N Street, NW, Suite 600
Washington, DC 20036-2479
Tel: 202-331-3500
http://www.asee.org

For information on engineering specialties and students clubs and competitions, contact
Junior Engineering Technical Society
1420 King Street, Suite 405
Alexandria, VA 22314-2750
Tel: 703-548-5387
E-mail: info@jets.org
http://www.jets.org

For information about careers, educational programs, scholarships, and student competitions, contact
Marine Technology Society
5565 Sterrett Place, Suite 108
Columbia, MD 21044-2606
Tel: 410-884-5330
http://www.mtsociety.org

For information on licensure and practice areas, contact
National Society of Professional Engineers
1420 King Street
Alexandria, VA 22314-2794
Tel: 703-684-2800
http://www.nspe.org

For information on licensure, contact
NCEES
280 Seneca Creek Road
Seneca, SC 29678-1405
Tel: 800-250-3196
http://www.ncees.org

For more information about ocean engineering, contact
Ocean Engineering Society
c/o Institute of Electrical and Electronics Engineers
http://www.oceanicengineering.org

For industry information, contact

Society of Naval Architects and Marine Engineers
601 Pavonia Avenue
Jersey City, NJ 07306-2922
Tel: 800-798-2188
http://www.sname.org

Physical Oceanographers

OVERVIEW

Oceanographers study the ocean by conducting observations, surveys, and experiments. *Physical oceanographers* are specialized oceanographers who study physical aspects of the ocean such as temperature and density; tides, waves, and currents; coastal erosion; and the relationship between the ocean and the atmosphere (for example, weather phenomena that affects the oceans such as temperature, wind, and rain).

HISTORY

Ocean currents, tides, winds, and waves have been observed and studied for thousands of years by traders, explorers, and scientists. Many people trace the origins of modern physical oceanography to the work of Matthew Fontaine Maury, a U.S. Navy Lieutenant. By analyzing logbooks kept by navy captains, Maury was able to create ocean charts. In 1855, he published *The Physical Geography of the Sea,* the first textbook on oceanography.

Although scientists and explorers had conducted research on the physical and chemical properties of the ocean for hundreds of years before, the ocean expedition of the HMS *Challenger* from 1872–76 marked the first comprehensive study of the sea—especially its lower depths. Expedition scientists traveled to every ocean except the Arctic to gather specimens and samples, take depth soundings, record deep-sea water temperatures, and conduct other research. The *Challenger*

Books to Read

Crane, Kathleen. *Sea Legs: Tales of a Woman Oceanographer.* New York: Basic Books, 2004.

DeGalan, Julie. *Great Jobs for Environmental Studies Majors.* 2d ed. New York: McGraw-Hill, 2008.

Garrison, Tom S. *Oceanography: An Invitation to Marine Science.* 7th ed. Stamford, Conn.: Brooks Cole, 2009.

Hamblin, Jacob Darwin. *Oceanographers and the Cold War: Disciples of Marine Science.* Seattle, Wash.: University of Washington Press, 2005.

Heitzmann, Ray. *Opportunities in Marine Science and Maritime Careers.* Rev. ed. New York: McGraw-Hill, 2006.

Knauss, John A. *Introduction to Physical Oceanography.* 2d ed. Long Grove, Ill.: Waveland Press Inc., 2005.

Miller, Charles B. *Biological Oceanography.* Malden, Mass.: Blackwell Publishers, 2004.

Millero, Frank J. *Chemical Oceanography.* 3d ed. Boca Raton, Fla.: CRC Press, 2005.

Parsons, Timothy, and Timothy Richard Parsons. *Sea's Enthrall: Memoirs of an Oceanographer.* Victoria, B.C., Canada: Trafford Publishing, 2007.

Trujillo, Alan P., and Harold V. Thurman. *Essentials of Oceanography.* 10th ed. Upper Saddle River, N.J.: Prentice Hall, 2010.

expedition allowed scientists to learn more about the oceans of the world than had ever been known.

From 1925 to 1927, a German research expedition aboard the *Meteor* studied the physical oceanography of the Atlantic Ocean. This expedition marked the beginning of the modern age of oceanographic investigation, according to *Invitation to Oceanography,* by Paul R. Pinet.

Today, physical oceanographers continue to conduct research via ocean expeditions, but also rely on technology such as satellites, acoustic measuring devices, underwater vehicles, computer- and satellite-linked floats and buoys, and ocean seismometers (an instrument that measures earth movement on the seafloor).

THE JOB

Physical oceanographers examine physical forces and features within the ocean. They observe and record the currents, temperatures, density, salinity, and acoustical characteristics of the ocean. Physical oceanographers are also concerned with the interaction between the ocean and the atmosphere, land, freshwater sources such as rivers, and the seafloor. A physical oceanographer might, for instance, try to determine how the ocean influences the climate or weather or affects a certain stretch of coastline.

Physical oceanographers gather data via visual observation, shipboard measurements, and programmable computer buoys, satellites, and other technologies. The development of satellites has allowed physical oceanographers to collect data more quickly than in the past. Physical oceanographers also use mathematical modeling software to help answer questions and form hypotheses (an educated guess) about the world's oceans. Some of the issues studied by physical oceanographers include weather and climate trends (including global warming), ocean pollution, the decline of ocean fisheries (which have crashed as a result of overfishing, pollution, and other factors), and algal blooms (often known as red tides) that can harm humans and ocean ecosystems.

Physical oceanographers work closely with biological, chemical, and geological oceanographers; atmospheric scientists; ocean engineers; and other marine scientists to conduct research and solve problems. One example of this cooperation can be found in the ECOHAB (Ecology and Oceanography of Harmful Algal Blooms) initiative. Physical oceanographers, biological oceanographers, and ocean engineers are currently studying harmful algal blooms in the Gulf of Maine caused by *Alexandrium* cells. The organism can cause paralytic shellfish poisoning. (Other marine scientists are conducting similar work in other areas of the world). According to Sea Grant Marine Careers, physical oceanographers are "assisting with oceanographic and satellite measurements, computer modeling, and instrument design, deployment, and recovery."

Physical oceanographers conduct observational research in the field and assess their findings and conduct experiments in laboratories and offices. Some work as college oceanography professors and write articles and books about their specialty.

REQUIREMENTS

High School

Because a college degree is required for a career in oceanography, you should take four years of college preparatory courses while in high school. Science courses, including geology, biology, and chemistry, and math classes, such as algebra, trigonometry, calculus, and statistics, are especially important to take. Because your work will involve a great deal of research and documentation, take English classes to improve your research and communication skills. In addition,

An oceanographer (*left*) and her team of students travel through the waters of Quartermaster Harbor off Vashon Island, Washington, as they study the aquatic organism *Alexandrium catenella*. The organism is responsible for producing red tide, which can cause toxic water conditions and make some marine organisms unsafe to eat. (*Dean J. Koepfler, AP Photo*/The News Tribune)

take computer science classes because you will be using computers throughout your professional life. Learning a foreign language will be useful—especially if you plan to work abroad.

Postsecondary Training

A bachelor's degree is the minimum educational requirement to enter the field, but most employers require a master's degree in oceanography, marine science, or a related field. A Ph.D. in oceanography is required for most positions in research and teaching. More than 100 institutions offer programs in marine studies, and more than 35 universities have graduate programs leading to a doctoral degree in oceanography.

Typical classes in a physical oceanography program include Principles of Physical Oceanography, Coastal and Estuarine Oceanography, Fluid Dynamics, Geophysical Fluid Dynamics, Theory of Ocean Circulation, Numerical Modeling in Ocean Circulation, Satellite Oceanography, and Special Topics in Physical Oceanography.

To prepare for graduate work, take mathematics through differential and integral calculus and at least one year each of chemistry and physics, biology or geology, and a modern foreign language.

Many oceanography students participate in internships or work as teaching assistants while in college to gain hands-on experience in the field. A list of internships is available at the American Society of Limnology and Oceanography's Web site, http://www.aslo.org.

Certification or Licensing
Oceanographers may scuba dive when conducting research. Organizations such as PADI provide basic certification (see For More Information for contact details).

Other Requirements
Personal traits helpful to a career in physical oceanography are a strong interest in science, particularly the physical and earth sciences; an interest in situations involving activities of an abstract and creative nature (observing nature and natural processes, performing experiments, creating objects); an interest in outdoor activities such as swimming or boating; an interest in scholarly activities (reading, researching, writing); and other interests that cut across the traditional academic boundaries of biology, chemistry, and physics. You should have above-average aptitudes in verbal, numerical, and spatial abilities. Other important skills include perseverance, integrity, open-mindedness, and attentiveness to detail.

EXPLORING

Visit Sea Grant's Marine Careers Web site (http://www.marine careers.net) for information on careers, volunteerships, internships, and other activities, such as sea camps. The Web sites of college oceanography departments offer a wealth of information about the field, typical classes, and internships. You may even be able to contact a professor or department head to ask a few questions about the career. If you are unable to contact a professor, ask your high school counselor to arrange an information interview with a physical oceanographer. You should also seek opportunities to gain firsthand oceanographic experience. Many coastal universities offer summer camp programs that enable young people to collect and analyze ocean data. You can help pave your way into the field by learning all you can about the geology, atmosphere, and plant and animal life of the area where you live, regardless of whether water is present.

EMPLOYERS

Oceanography jobs can be found all over the United States, and not just where the water meets the shore. Although the majority of jobs are on the Pacific, Atlantic, and Gulf coasts, many other jobs are available to the marine scientist. Universities, colleges, and federal and state agencies are the largest employers of physical oceanographers.

Other employers of physical oceanographers include international organizations, private companies, consulting firms, nonprofit laboratories, and local governments. Sometimes oceanographers are self-employed as consultants with their own businesses.

STARTING OUT

Most college career services offices are staffed to help you find positions with government agencies and in the private sector after you graduate. Often positions can be found through your college's career services office by application and interview. College and university assistantships, instructorships, and professorships are usually obtained by recommendation of your major professor or department chairperson. In addition, internships with the government or private industry during college can often lead to permanent employment after graduation. Additionally, the Marine Technology Society, American Society of Limnology and Oceanography, and The Oceanography Society offer job listings at their Web sites.

ADVANCEMENT

Starting physical oceanography positions for those with a bachelor's degree usually involve working as a laboratory or research assistant, with on-the-job training in applying oceanographic principles to the problems at hand. Some beginning oceanographers with Ph.D.'s may qualify for college teaching or research positions. Experienced personnel, particularly those with advanced graduate work or doctorates, can become supervisors or administrators. Such positions involve considerable responsibility in planning and policymaking or policy interpretation. Those who achieve top-level oceanographer positions may plan and supervise research projects involving a number of workers, or they may be in charge of an oceanographic laboratory or aquarium.

EARNINGS

Salaries for geoscientists (an occupational group that includes geologists, geophysicists, and oceanographers) ranged from less than

$43,140 to more than $161,260 in 2009, according to the U.S. Department of Labor. The median salary was $81,220. Experienced oceanographers working for the federal government earned $105,671 in 2009.

In addition to their regular salaries, oceanographers may supplement their incomes with fees earned from consulting, lecturing, and publishing their findings. As highly trained scientists, oceanographers usually enjoy good benefits, such as health insurance and retirement plans offered by their employers.

WORK ENVIRONMENT

Physical oceanographers conduct research on a research vessel, on a beach, in a laboratory, or at a desk. While oceanographers spend the majority of their time on land analyzing data, many also go to sea at least once or twice each year. One two-week research cruise can provide an oceanographer with enough data to study for an entire year. While at sea, physical oceanographers must live on board a ship in tight quarters with other scientists and support staff. They work in all types of weather—from rough seas caused by storms or high winds, to extreme cold and snow, to blazing sun in tropical climates. Some oceanographers may also conduct research in the ocean by donning scuba gear or journeying to the ocean depths in underwater vehicles.

Physical oceanographers who work in a laboratory or office typically work five-day, 40-hour weeks. They may have to occasionally work longer hours when conducting and observing certain research experiments. Facilities are typically clean and well lit.

Physical oceanographers who work in colleges or universities have a regular school calendar, with summers and breaks off for travel or research.

OUTLOOK

Employment for all geoscientists (including oceanographers) will grow faster than the average for all occupations through 2018, according to the U.S. Department of Labor. Despite this prediction, competition for top positions will be strong. Although job availability is difficult to predict for several years out, anyone doing good, strong academic work with a well-known professor in the field will have good employment chances. Additionally, oceanographers who speak a foreign language, have advanced degrees, and are willing to work abroad will have good employment prospects.

FOR MORE INFORMATION

For education and career information, contact the following organizations:

Acoustical Society of America
Two Huntington Quadrangle, Suite 1NO1
Melville, NY 11747-4502
Tel: 516-576-2360
E-mail: asa@aip.org
http://asa.aip.org

American Geophysical Union
2000 Florida Avenue, NW
Washington, DC 20009-1277
Tel: 800-966-2481
http://www.agu.org

This organization for diving scientists stresses diving safety and offers internships for college students.

American Academy of Underwater Sciences
Dauphin Island Sea Lab
101 Bienville Boulevard
Dauphin Island, AL 36528-4603
Tel: 251-591-3775
E-mail: aaus@disl.org
http://www.aaus.org

The Education section of the institute's Web site has information on careers in biology.

American Institute of Biological Sciences
1444 I Street, NW, Suite 200
Washington, DC 20005-6535
Tel: 202-628-1500
http://www.aibs.org

Visit the society's Web site for information on careers and education.

American Society of Limnology and Oceanography
5400 Bosque Boulevard, Suite 680
Waco, TX 76710-4446
Tel: 800-929-2756
E-mail: business@aslo.org
http://www.aslo.org
http://www.mtsociety.org

For links to career information and sea programs, visit the following Web sites:

Careers in Oceanography, Marine Science, and Marine Biology
http://ocean.peterbrueggeman.com/career.html

Sea Grant Marine Careers
http://www.marinecareers.net

WomenOceanographers.org
http://www.womenoceanographers.org

For information about careers, educational programs, scholarships, and student competitions, contact

Marine Technology Society
5565 Sterrett Place, Suite 108
Columbia, MD 21044-2606
Tel: 410-884-5330
http://www.mtsociety.org

For information on oceanography, contact

National Oceanic and Atmospheric Administration
U.S. Department of Commerce
1401 Constitution Avenue, NW, Room 5128
Washington, DC 20230-0001
http://www.noaa.gov

Contact this society for ocean news and information on membership.

The Oceanography Society
PO Box 1931
Rockville, MD 20849-1931
Tel: 301-251-7708
E-mail: info@tos.org
http://www.tos.org

For information on diving instruction and certification, contact

Professional Association of Diving Instructors (PADI)
30151 Tomas Street
Rancho Santa Margarita, CA 92688-2125
Tel: 800-729-7234
http://www.padi.com

Science Writers and Editors

QUICK FACTS

School Subjects
Biology
Earth science
English

Personal Skills
Communication/ideas
Technical/scientific

Work Environment
Indoors and outdoors
Primarily multiple locations

Minimum Education Level
Bachelor's degree

Salary Range
$28,070 to $53,900 to
$105,710+ (writers)
$28,430 to $50,800 to
$97,360+ (editors)

Certification or Licensing
None available

Outlook
About as fast as the average

DOT
131, 132

GOE
01.02.01

NOC
5121, 5122

O*NET-SOC
27-3041.00, 27-3042.00,
27-3043.00

OVERVIEW

Science writers translate technical scientific information so it can be disseminated to the general public and professionals in the field. They research, interpret, write, and edit scientific information. Their work often appears in books, technical studies and reports, magazine and trade journal articles, newspapers, company newsletters, and on Web sites and may be used for radio and television broadcasts. Other science writers work as *public information officers* for zoos, aquariums, museums, and government science agencies.

Science editors perform a wide range of functions, but their primary responsibility is to ensure that text provided by science writers is suitable in content, format, and style for the intended audiences. Readers are an editor's first priority.

HISTORY

The skill of writing has existed for thousands of years. Papyrus fragments with writing by ancient Egyptians date from about 3000 B.C., and archaeological findings show that the Chinese had developed books by about 1300 B.C.

The history of book editing is tied closely to the history of the book and bookmaking and the history of the printing process. In the early days of publishing, authors worked directly with the printer, and the printer was often the publisher and seller of the author's work. Eventually, however, booksellers began to work directly with the authors and eventually took over the role of publisher. The publisher then became the middleman between author and printer. The publisher worked closely with the author and sometimes acted as the editor; the word *editor,* in fact, derives from the Latin word *edere* or *editum* and means supervising or directing the preparation of text. Eventually, specialists were hired to perform the editing function. These editors, who were also called advisers or literary advisers in the 19th century, became an integral part of the publishing business.

The editor, also called the sponsor in some houses, sought out the best authors, worked with them, and became their advocate in the publishing house. So important did some editors become that their very presence in a publishing house could determine the quality of author that might be published there. The field has grown through the 20th and 21st centuries, with computers greatly speeding up the process by which editors prepare text for the printer or electronic publication.

The broadcasting industry has also contributed to the development of the professional writer. Film, radio, and television are sources of entertainment, information, and education that provide employment for thousands of writers. Today, the computer industry and Internet Web sites have also created the need for more writers.

Oceans and marine life have been studied since ancient times. *Historia Animalium,* the first treatise on marine biology, was written by the philosopher Aristotle in 325 B.C. By the late 1600s, books, journals, logbooks, articles, and other written summaries about ocean exploration trips and studies of marine life became important tools for scientists, the maritime industry, and, occasionally, the general public. Noteworthy publications of the 17th through 19th centuries include *Observations and Experiments on the Saltiness of the Sea,* by Robert Boyle (1674); *Histoire Physique de la Mer* (considered to be the first book that dealt entirely with the science of the oceans), by Luigi Marsigli (1725); *Distribution of Marine Life,* by Sir Edward Forbes (1854); *The Physical Geography of the Sea,* by Matthew Fontaine Maury (1855); the *Challenger Reports* (a more than 50-volume summary of the groundbreaking HMS *Challenger* expedition that was conducted from 1872 to 1876); and *The Depths of the Sea,* by Charles Wyville Thomson (1876).

As oceanography grew into a distinct discipline in the 1920s, more writers and editors began crafting books and articles about oceanographical discoveries for scientists, students, and the general public. Today, a basic search on the Internet or in a library database will turn up thousands of books about the field.

As our world becomes more complex and people seek even more information, professional writers have become increasingly important. And, as science take giant steps forward and discoveries are being made every day that impact our lives and allow us to better understand our world's oceans, skilled science writers are needed to document these changes and disseminate the information to the general public and more specialized audiences.

THE JOB

Science writers usually write for the general public. They translate scientific information into articles and reports that the general public and the media can understand. They might write about global warming and its effects on coastal communities, the disease-fighting properties of a newly discovered marine plant, global efforts to fight pollution, an endangered species of dolphin or seal, and countless other topics. Good writers who cover the subjects thoroughly have inquisitive minds and enjoy looking for additional information that might add to their articles. They research the topic to gain a thorough understanding of the subject matter. This may require hours of research on the Internet; in corporate, university, or public libraries; at zoos and aquariums; or out in the natural world on a research vessel or the coastline. Writers always need good background information regarding a subject before they can write about it.

In order to get the information required, writers may interview environmental scientists (such as oceanographers, marine biologists, etc.), engineers, politicians, and others who are familiar with the subject. Writers must know how to present the information so it can be understood. This requires knowing the audience and how to reach them. For example, an article on tsunamis may need graphs, photos, or historical facts. Writers sometimes enlist the help of technical illustrators or engineers in order to add a visual dimension to their work.

For instance, if reporting on a tsunami that has killed thousands of people in the Pacific, writers will need to illustrate the factors that cause a tsunami (earthquakes, but also underwater landslides, volcanic eruptions, and even very rarely the impact of a large meteorite in the ocean). The public will also want to know what areas of the earth are affected by tsunamis (coastal areas), what the warning signs are (a recent earthquake in the region, suddenly receding waters from coastal areas, etc.), and what governments are doing to prepare their citizens for tsunamis (educating the public about warning signs of tsunamis, creating early warning networks among tsunami-threatened nations, etc.). In addition, interviews with scientists and tsunami survivors add a personal touch to the story.

Writers usually need to work quickly because news-related stores are often deadline-oriented. Because science can be so complex, science writers also need to help the audience understand and evaluate the information. Writing for the Web encompasses most journalistic guidelines, including time constraints and sometimes space constraints.

Some science writers specialize in their subject matter. For instance, a science writer may write only about marine biology and earn a reputation as the best writer in that subject area. Or they may limit their writing or research to writing about pollution, or may be even more specific and focus only on water pollution issues.

Some writers may choose to be freelance writers either on a full- or part-time basis, or to supplement other jobs. Freelance science writers are self-employed writers who work with small and large companies, research institutions, or publishing firms on a contract or hourly basis. They may specialize in writing about a specific scientific subject for one or two clients, or they may write about a broad range of subjects for a number of different clients. Many freelance writers write articles, papers, or reports and then attempt to get them published in newspapers, trade, or consumer publications.

Editors work for many kinds of publishers, publications, and corporations. Editors' titles vary widely, not only from one area of publishing to another but also within each area. *Book editors* prepare written material for publication. In small publishing houses, the same editor may guide the material through all the stages of the publishing process. They may work with printers, designers, advertising agencies, and other members of the publishing industry. In larger publishing houses, editors tend to be more specialized, being involved in only a part of the publishing process.

Acquisitions editors are the editors who find new writers and sign on new projects. They are responsible for finding new ideas for books that will sell well and for finding writers who can create the books.

Production editors are responsible for taking the manuscript written by an author and polishing the work into a finished print or electronic publication. They correct grammar, spelling, and style, and check all the facts. They make sure the book reads well and suggest changes to the author if it does not. The production editor may be responsible for getting the cover designed and the art put into a book. Because the work is so demanding, production editors usually work on only one or two books at a time.

Copy editors assist the production editor in polishing the author's writing. Copy editors review each page and make all the changes required to give the book a good writing style. *Line editors* review the text to make sure specific style rules are obeyed. They make sure the same spelling is used for words where more than one spelling is correct (for example, grey and gray). *Fact checkers* and *proofreaders* read the manuscript to make sure everything is spelled correctly and that all the facts in the text have been checked.

The basic functions performed by *magazine* and *newspaper editors* are much like those performed by book editors, but a significant amount of the writing that appears in magazines and newspapers, or periodicals, is done by *staff writers*. Periodicals often use editors who specialize in specific areas, such as *city editors,* who oversee the work of reporters who specialize in local news, and *department editors*. Department editors specialize in areas such as business, fashion, sports, and features, to name only a few. These departments are determined by the interests of the audience that the periodical intends to reach. Like book houses, periodicals use copy editors, researchers, and fact checkers, but at small periodicals, one or a few editors may be responsible for tasks that would be performed by many people at a larger publication.

REQUIREMENTS

High School

If you are considering a career as a writer or editor, you should take English, journalism, and communication courses in high school. Computer classes will also be helpful. If you know in high school that you want to do scientific writing or editing, it would be to your advantage to take biology, physiology, earth science, chemistry, physics, math, and other science-related courses. If your school offers journalism courses and you have the chance to work on the school newspaper or yearbook, you should take advantage of these opportunities. Part-time employment at newspapers, publishing companies, or scientific research facilities can also provide experience and insight regarding this career.

Postsecondary Training

Although not all writers and editors are college-educated, today's jobs almost always require a bachelor's degree. Many writers earn an undergraduate degree in English, journalism, or liberal arts and then obtain a master's degree in a communications field such as writing. A good liberal arts education is important since you are often required to write about many subject areas. Science-related courses (or even pursuing a science-related field, such as marine biology, oceanography, or environmental science, as a second major) are highly recommended. You should investigate internship programs that give you experience in the communications department of a corporation, environmental firm, government agency, or research facility. Some newspapers, magazines, or public relations firms also have internships that give you the opportunity to write and work as an editor.

Some people find that after working as a writer, their interests are strong in the science field and they evolve into that writing specialty.

Did You Know?

- Oceans cover about 72 percent of the planet's surface—or 140 million square miles.
- The average depth of the ocean is 12,200 feet.
- Approximately 80 percent of all life on Earth lives in the ocean.
- The surface temperature of oceans ranges from about 86°F at the equator to about 29°F near the poles. The world's warmest water is in the Persian Gulf, where surface temperatures of 96°F have been recorded.
- Less than 10 percent of the deepest parts of the ocean, called the abyss or abyssal plain, have been explored.
- It is estimated that there are at least 100 million unnamed species living on the floor of the ocean.
- More than 3.5 billion people rely on the ocean as their main source of food.
- Coral reefs make up less than .02 percent of the ocean's bottom, but contain more than 25 percent of all life in the sea.
- Approximately 10 percent of coral reefs have been destroyed and about 60 percent are in danger of being killed.
- Human development, global warming, pollution, and hurricanes are the biggest threats to coral reefs.
- The ocean absorbs nearly two billion tons of carbon dioxide each year; if not absorbed, this gas would be extremely harmful to our environment.
- Less than 0.5 percent of marine habitats are protected. More than 11 percent of land is protected.

Source: SavetheSea.org, MarineBio.com, Exploring the Environment: Coral Reefs

They may return to school and enter a master's degree program or take some additional courses related specifically to science writing. Similarly, science majors may find that they like the writing aspect of their jobs and return to school to pursue a career as a science writer.

Other Requirements

Writers and editors should be creative and able to express ideas clearly, have an interest in science, be skilled in research techniques, and be computer literate. Other assets include curiosity, persistence, initiative, resourcefulness, and an accurate memory. For some jobs—on a newspaper, for example, where the activity is hectic and deadlines short—the ability to concentrate and produce under pressure is essential.

You must be detail oriented to succeed as a writer or an editor. You must also be patient, since you may have to spend hours synthesizing information into the written or electronic word or turning a few pages of near-gibberish into powerful, elegant English. If you are the kind of person who can't sit still, you probably will not succeed in these careers. To be a good writer or editor, you must be a self-starter who is not afraid to make decisions. You must be good not only at identifying problems but also at solving them, so you must be creative.

EXPLORING

As a high school or college student, you can test your interest and aptitude in the field of writing and editing by serving as a reporter or writer on school newspapers, yearbooks, and literary magazines. Attending writing workshops and taking writing classes will give you the opportunity to practice and sharpen your skills. Practice editing your own work or the work of friends to get a basic introduction of what it takes to work as an editor.

Community newspapers often welcome contributions from outside sources, although they may not have the resources to pay for them. Jobs in bookstores, magazine shops, libraries, and even newsstands offer a chance to become familiar with various publications. If you are interested in science writing or editing, try to get a part-time job in a research laboratory, interview science writers and editors, and read good science writing in major newspapers such as the *New York Times* or in publications published by major science associations.

Information on writing as a career may also be obtained by visiting local newspapers and publishing houses and interviewing some of the writers and editors who work there. Career conferences and other guidance programs frequently include speakers from local or national organizations who can provide information on communication careers.

Some professional organizations such as the Society for Technical Communication welcome students as members and have special student membership rates and career information. In addition, participation in professional organizations gives you the opportunity to meet and visit with people in this career field.

EMPLOYERS

Many science writers and editors are employed, often on a freelance basis, by newspaper, magazine, and book publishers, and the broadcast industries as well. Internet publishing is a growing field that hires science writers and editors. Science writers and editors are also employed by scientific research companies; government research facilities; federal, state, and local government agencies; and research and development departments of corporations. Large colleges and universities often employ science writers and editors in their public relations departments and as writing professors. Zoos, aquariums, museums, and government agencies also employ writers as public information officers.

STARTING OUT

A fair amount of experience is required to gain a high-level position in this field. Most writers start out in entry-level positions. These jobs may be listed with college career services offices, or you may apply directly to the employment departments of publishing companies, corporations, institutions, universities, research facilities, nonprofit organizations, and government facilities that hire science writers. Many firms now hire writers directly upon application or recommendation of college professors and career services offices. Want ads in newspapers and trade journals are another source for jobs. Serving an internship in college can give you the advantage of knowing people who can give you personal recommendations.

Internships are also excellent ways to build your portfolio. Employers in the communications field are usually interested in seeing samples of your published writing assembled in an organized portfolio or scrapbook. Working on your college's magazine or newspaper staff can help you build a portfolio. Sometimes small, regional, or local magazines and newspapers will also buy articles or assign short pieces for you to write. You should attempt to build your portfolio with good writing samples. Be sure to include the type of writing you are interested in doing, if possible.

You may need to begin your career as a junior writer or editor and work your way up. This usually involves library research, preparation of rough drafts for part or all of a report, cataloging, and other related writing tasks. These are generally carried on under the supervision of a senior writer.

Many science writers enter the field after working in public relations departments or science-related industries. They may use their skills to transfer to specialized writing positions or they may take additional courses or graduate work that focuses on writing or documentation skills.

There is tremendous competition for editorial jobs, so it is important for a beginner who wishes to break into the business to be as well prepared as possible. College students who have gained experience as interns, have worked for publications during summer vacations, or have attended special programs in publishing will be at an advantage. In addition, applicants for any editorial position must be extremely careful when preparing cover letters and resumes. Even a single error in spelling or usage will disqualify an applicant. Applicants for editorial or proofreading positions must also expect to take and pass tests that are designed to determine their language skills.

Many editors enter the field as editorial assistants or proofreaders. Some editorial assistants perform only clerical tasks, whereas others may also proofread or perform basic editorial tasks. Typically, an editorial assistant who performs well will be given the opportunity to take on more and more editorial duties as time passes. Proofreaders have the advantage of being able to look at the work of editors, so they can learn while they do their own work.

Good sources of information about job openings are school career services offices, classified ads in newspapers and trade journals, specialized publications such as *Publishers Weekly* (http://publishersweekly.com), and Internet sites. One way to proceed is to identify local publishers through the Yellow Pages. Many publishers have Web sites that list job openings, and large publishers often have telephone job lines that serve the same purpose.

ADVANCEMENT

Writers with only an undergraduate degree may choose to earn a graduate degree in science writing, corporate communications, graphic design, or a related program. An advanced degree may open doors to more progressive career options.

Many experienced science writers are often promoted to head writing, documentation, or public relations departments within corporations or institutions. Some may become recognized experts in their field and their writings may be in demand by trade journals, newspapers, magazines, and the broadcast industry. Writers employed by newspapers and magazines may advance by working for larger, more prestigious publications.

As freelance writers prove themselves and work successfully with clients, they may be able to demand increased contract fees or hourly rates.

In book publishing houses, employees who start as editorial assistants or proofreaders and show promise generally become copy editors. After gaining skill in that position, they may be given a wider range of duties while retaining the same title. The next step may be a position as a *senior copy editor,* which involves overseeing the work of junior copy editors, or as a project editor. The *project editor* performs a wide variety of tasks, including copyediting, coordinating the work of in-house and freelance copy editors, and managing the schedule of a particular project. From this position, an editor may move up to become *first assistant editor,* then *managing editor,* then *editor in chief.* These positions involve more management and decision making than is usually found in the positions described previously. The editor in chief works with the publisher to ensure that a suitable editorial policy is being followed, while the managing editor is responsible for all aspects of the editorial department. The assistant editor provides support to the managing editor.

Newspaper editors generally begin working on the copy desk, where they progress from less significant stories and projects to major news and feature stories. A common route to advancement is for copy editors to be promoted to a particular department, where they may move up the ranks to management positions. An editor who has achieved success in a department may become a city editor, who is responsible for news, or a managing editor, who runs the entire editorial operation of a newspaper.

The advancement path for magazine editors is similar to that of book editors. After they become copy editors, they work their way up to become senior editors, managing editors, and editors in chief. In many cases, magazine editors advance by moving from a position on one magazine to the same position with a larger or more prestigious magazine. Such moves often bring significant increases in both pay and status.

EARNINGS

Although there are no specific salary studies for science writers, salary information for all writers is available. The U.S. Department of Labor (DOL) reports that the mean annual salary for writers was

$53,900 in 2009. Salaries ranged from less than $28,070 to more than $105,710. Mean annual earnings for writers employed by newspaper, book, and directory publishers were $53,050 in 2009.

The DOL reports that the median annual earnings for all editors were $50,800 in 2009. Salaries ranged from $28,430 or less to more than $97,360. Those who worked for newspaper, periodical, book, and directory publishers earned annual salaries of $58,580.

Freelance writers' and editors' earnings can vary depending on their expertise, reputation, and the articles they are contracted to write.

Most full-time writing and editing positions offer the usual benefits such as insurance, sick leave, and paid vacation. Some jobs also provide tuition reimbursement and retirement benefits. Freelance writers must pay for their own insurance. However, there are professional associations that may offer group insurance rates for their members.

WORK ENVIRONMENT

Work environment depends on the type of science writing and the employer. Generally, writers work in an office or research environment. Writers for the news media sometimes work in noisy surroundings. Some writers travel to research information and conduct interviews while other employers may confine research to local libraries or the Internet. In addition, some employers require writers to conduct research interviews over the phone, rather than in person.

Although the workweek usually runs 35 to 40 hours in a normal office setting, many writers may have to work overtime to cover a story, interview people, meet deadlines, or to disseminate information in a timely manner. The newspaper and broadcasting industries deliver the news 24 hours a day, seven days a week. Writers often work nights and weekends to meet press deadlines or to cover a late-developing story.

Each day may bring new and interesting situations. Some stories may even take writers to remote and exotic locales. Other assignments may be boring or they may take place in less than desirable settings, where interview subjects may be rude, busy, and unwilling to talk or conditions may be cold, snowy, rainy, or otherwise uncomfortable. One of the most difficult elements for writers may be meeting deadlines or gathering information. People who are the most content as writers work well with deadline pressure.

The environments in which editors work vary widely. For the most part, publishers of all kinds realize that a quiet atmosphere is conducive to work that requires tremendous concentration. It takes an unusual ability to focus to edit in a noisy place. Most editors work in private offices or cubicles. Book editors often work in quieter surroundings than do newspaper editors or quality-control people in advertising agencies, who sometimes work in rather loud and hectic situations.

Even in relatively quiet surroundings, however, editors often have many distractions. A project editor who is trying to do some copyediting or review the editing of others may, for example, have to deal with phone calls from authors, questions from junior editors, meetings with members of the editorial and production staff, and questions from freelancers, among many other distractions.

Deadlines are an important issue for virtually all editors. Newspaper and magazine editors work in a much more pressurized atmosphere than book editors because they face daily or weekly deadlines, whereas book production usually takes place over several months.

In almost all cases, editors must work long hours during certain phases of the editing process. Some newspaper editors start work at 5 A.M., others work until 11 P.M. or even through the night. Feature editors, columnists, and editorial page editors usually can schedule their day in a more regular fashion, as can editors who work on weekly newspapers. Editors working on hard news, however, may receive an assignment that must be completed, even if work extends well into the next shift.

OUTLOOK

According to the U.S. Department of Labor, there is strong competition for writing and editing jobs, and growth in writing careers should occur at an average rate through 2018. Opportunities will be good for science writers and editors, as discoveries in the natural world, including the oceans, will drive the need for skilled writers to put complex scientific information in terms that a wide and varied audience can understand.

FOR MORE INFORMATION

ACES is an excellent source of information about careers in copyediting. It organizes educational seminars and maintains lists of internships.
   American Copy Editors Society (ACES)
   http://www.copydesk.org

ASNE helps editors maintain the highest standards of quality, improve their craft, and better serve their communities. It preserves and promotes core journalistic values.

American Society of News Editors (ASNE)
11690B Sunrise Valley Drive
Reston, VA 20191-1436
Tel: 703-453-1122
http://www.asne.org

For information on membership, contact
Association of Earth Science Editors
http://www.aese.org

For information on careers in science writing, contact
Council for the Advancement of Science Writing
PO Box 910
Hedgesville, WV 25427-0910
Tel: 304-754-6786
http://www.casw.org

To read advice for beginning science writers, visit the NASW Web site.
National Association of Science Writers (NASW)
PO Box 7905
Berkeley, CA 94707-0905
Tel: 510-647-9500
http://www.nasw.org

For information about working as a writer and union membership, contact
National Writers Union
256 West 38th Street, Suite 703
New York, NY 10018-9807
Tel: 212-254-0279
http://www.nwu.org

For information on scholarships and student memberships aimed at those preparing for a career in technical communication, contact
Society for Technical Communication
9401 Lee Highway, Suite 300
Fairfax, VA 22031-1803
Tel: 703-522-4114
E-mail: stc@src.org
http://www.stc.org

For a wide range of resources relating to environmental journalism, contact

Society of Environmental Journalists
PO Box 2492
Jenkintown, PA 19046-8492
Tel: 215-884-8174
E-mail: sej@sej.org
http://www.sej.org

This organization for journalists has campus and online chapters.
Society of Professional Journalists
Eugene S. Pulliam National Journalism Center
3909 North Meridian Street
Indianapolis, IN 46208-4011
Tel: 317-927-8000
http://www.spj.org

Zoo and Aquarium Curators

QUICK FACTS

School Subjects
Biology
Business
Speech

Personal Skills
Communication/ideas
Technical/scientific

Work Environment
Indoors and outdoors
Primarily one location

Minimum Education Level
Bachelor's degree

Salary Range
$27,000 to $47,930 to
$83,900+

Certification or Licensing
None available

Outlook
More slowly than the average

DOT
102

GOE
12.03.04

NOC
0212

O*NET-SOC
25-4012.00

OVERVIEW

Zoos are wild kingdoms, and aquariums are underwater worlds. The word *zoo* comes from the Greek for "living being" and is a shortened term for zoological garden or zoological park; although this may imply that zoos are created just for beauty and recreation, the main functions of modern zoos are education, conservation, and the study of animals. The term *aquarium* comes from the Latin for "source of water"; in such places, living aquatic plants and animals are studied and exhibited. These land and water gardens are tended by people with an affinity for animals. *Zoo and aquarium curators* are the chief employees responsible for the care of the creatures found at these public places; they oversee the various sections of the animal collections, such as birds, mammals, and fishes.

There are approximately 11,100 curators employed in the United States. Only a small percentage of this total work at zoos and aquariums.

HISTORY

Prehistoric humans did not try to tame animals; for purposes of survival, they hunted them to avoid danger as well as to obtain food. The full history of the establishment of zoos and aquariums can be traced probably as far back as the earliest attempts by humans to domesticate animals after realizing that they could live with them as fellow creatures. The precise timing of this phenomenon is not known; it apparently occurred at different times in different parts of the world.

Ancient Sumerians kept fish in man-made ponds around 4,500 years ago. By 1150 B.C., pigeons, elephants, antelope, and deer were held captive for taming in such areas as the Middle East, India, and China. In 1000 B.C., a Chinese emperor named Wen Wang built a zoo and called it the Garden of Intelligence. Also around this time, the Chinese and Japanese were breeding and raising goldfish and carp for their beauty.

Zoos were abundant in ancient Greece; animals were held in captivity for purposes of study in nearly every city-state. In early Egypt and Asia, zoos were created mainly for public show, and during the Roman Empire, fish were kept in ponds and animals were collected both for arena showings and for private zoos. A fantastic zoo, with 300 keepers taking care of birds, mammals, and reptiles, was created in Mexico in the early 16th century by Hernando Cortes, the Spanish conqueror.

Zoo and aquarium professions as we know them today began to be established around the mid-18th century with the construction of various extravagant European zoos. The Imperial Menagerie of the Schönbrunn Zoo in Vienna, Austria, was opened in 1765 and still operates to this day. One of the most significant openings occurred in 1828 at the London Zoological Society's Regent's Park. The world's first public aquarium was also established at Regent's Park, in 1853, after which aquariums were built in other European cities. In the United States, P. T. Barnum was the first to establish a display aquarium, which opened in New York in 1856.

Of the aquariums located in most large cities throughout the world, the largest research facilities include the Oceanographic Institute (Monaco) and the Scripps Institution of Oceanography (California). Commercial aquariums include Sea World (Orlando, Florida; San Diego, California; and San Antonio, Texas) and the Miami Seaquarium (Florida), which show fish in tanks that hold as much as 1 million gallons of water.

Today, curators have a host of responsibilities involved with the operation of zoos and aquariums. Although many zoos and aquariums are separate places, there are also zoos that contain aquariums as part of their facilities. There are both public and private institutions, large and small, and curators often contribute their knowledge to the most effective methods of design, maintenance, and administration for these institutions.

THE JOB

General curators of zoos and aquariums oversee the management of an institution's entire animal collection and animal management staff. They help the director coordinate activities, such as education, collection planning, exhibit design, new construction, research, and public services. They meet with the director and other members of the staff to create long-term strategic plans. General curators may have public relations and development responsibilities, such as meeting with the media and identifying and cultivating donors. In most institutions, general curators develop policy; other curators implement policy.

Animal curators are responsible for the day-to-day management of a specific portion of a zoo's or aquarium's animal collection (as defined taxonomically, such as mammals or birds, or ecogeographically, such as the tidal pool); the people charged with caring for that collection, including assistant curators, aquarists, zookeepers, administrative staff such as secretaries, as well as researchers, students, and volunteers; and the associated facilities and equipment.

For example, the curator in charge of the marine mammal department of a large zoo would be responsible for the care of such animals as sea lions, dolphins, manatees, polar bears, sea and marine otters, and walrus. He or she might oversee more than 100 animals, representing nearly 120 different species, manage scores of employees, and have a multimillion dollar budget.

Assistant curators report to curators and assist in animal management tasks and decisions. They may have extensive supervisory responsibilities.

Curators have diverse responsibilities and their activities vary widely from day to day. They oversee animal husbandry procedures, including the daily care of the animals, establish proper nutritional programs, and manage animal health delivery in partnership with the veterinary staff. They develop exhibits, educational programs, and visitor services and participate in research and conservation activities. They maintain inventories of animals and other records, and they recommend and implement acquisitions and dispositions of animals. Curators serve as liaisons with other departments.

Curators prepare budgets and reports. They interview and hire new workers. When scientific conferences are held, curators attend them as representatives of the institutions for which they work. They are often called upon to write articles for scientific journals and perhaps provide information for newspaper reports and magazine stories. They may coordinate or participate in on-site research or conservation efforts. To keep abreast with developments in their field, curators spend a lot of time reading.

Curators meet with the general curator, the director, and other staff to develop the objectives and philosophy of the institution

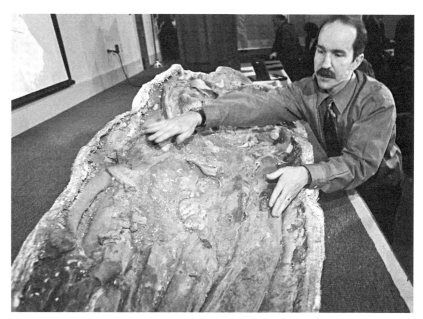

The curator of paleontology at the Calvert Marine Museum in Solomons, Maryland, shows the remains of an 8-million-year-old baline whale fossil. The fossil was discovered after a hurricane eroded the coastline along the St. Mary's River in St. Mary's County, Maryland. (*Matt Houston, AP Photo*)

and decide on the best way to care for and exhibit the animals. They must be knowledgeable about the animals' housing requirements, daily care, medical procedures, dietary needs, and social and reproduction habits. Curators represent their zoos or aquariums in collaborative efforts with other institutions, such as the more than 110 Association of Zoos and Aquariums (AZA) Species Survival Plans that target individual species for intense conservation efforts by zoos and aquariums. In this capacity, curators may exchange information, negotiate breeding loans, or assemble the necessary permits and paperwork to effect the transfers. Other methods of animal acquisition coordinated by curators involve purchases from animal dealers or private collectors and collection of nonendangered species from the wild. Curators may arrange for the quarantine of newly acquired animals. They may arrange to send the remains of dead animals to museums or universities for study.

Curators often work on special projects. They may serve on multidisciplinary committees responsible for planning and constructing new exhibits. Curators interface with colleagues from other states and around the world in collaborative conservation efforts.

Although most zoo and aquarium curators check on the collection on a regular basis, they are usually more involved with administrative issues than animal husbandry. Much of their time is spent in meetings or writing e-mails or on talking on the phone.

In addition to animal curators, large institutions employ curators whose responsibilities involve areas other than animal husbandry, such as research, conservation, exhibits, horticulture, and education.

REQUIREMENTS

High School
High school students who want to prepare for careers in upper management in zoos and aquariums should take classes in the sciences, especially biology, microbiology, chemistry, and physics, as well as in business, mathematics, computer science, English, and speech.

Postsecondary Training
The minimum formal educational requirement for curators is a bachelor's degree in one of the biological sciences, such as zoology, ecology, biology, oceanography, mammalogy, and ornithology. Course work should include biology, invertebrate zoology, vertebrate physiology, comparative anatomy, organic chemistry, physics, microbiology, and virology. Electives are just as important, particularly writing, public speaking, computer science, and education. Even studying a second language can be helpful.

Typically, an advanced degree is required for curators employed at most institutions—many employers require curators to have a doctoral degree. But advanced academic training alone is insufficient; it takes years of on-the-job experience to master the practical aspects of exotic animal husbandry. Also required are management skills, supervisory experience, writing ability, research experience, and sometimes the flexibility to travel.

A few institutions offer curatorial internships designed to provide practical experience. Several major zoos offer formal keeper training courses as well as on-the-job training programs to students who are studying areas related to animal science and care. Such programs could lead to positions as assistant curators. Contact the AZA for further information about which schools and animal facilities are involved in internship programs.

Other Requirements
Curators who work for zoos and aquariums must have a fondness and compassion for animals. But as managers of people, strong

interpersonal skills are extremely important for curators, including conflict management and negotiating. Curators spend a lot of time making deals with people inside and outside of their institutions. They must have recognized leadership ability, good coaching skills, and the ability to create and maintain a team atmosphere and build consensus.

Curators also need excellent oral and written communication skills. They must be effective and articulate public speakers. They need to be good at problem solving.

Curators should have an in-depth knowledge of every species and exhibit in their collections and how they interact. Modern zoo and aquarium buildings contain technologically advanced, complex equipment, such as environmental controls, and often house mixed-species exhibits. Not only must curators know about zoology and animal husbandry, but they must understand the infrastructure as well.

EXPLORING

Reading about animals or surfing the Internet, taking classes at local zoos and aquariums, or joining clubs, such as 4-H or Audubon, can help students learn about animals. Taking time to learn about ecology and nature in general will prepare students for the systems-oriented approach used by modern zoo and aquarium managers.

Volunteering at zoos or aquariums, animal shelters, wildlife rehabilitation facilities, stables, or veterinary hospitals demonstrates a serious commitment to animals and provides firsthand experience with them.

Professional organizations, such as AZA and the American Association of Zoo Keepers, Inc. (AAZK), have special membership rates for nonprofessionals. Associate members receive newsletters and can attend workshops and conferences.

EMPLOYERS

Because there are so few zoos and aquariums in North America (approximately 215), most positions will be the result of turnover, which is low. While a few new zoos and aquariums may open and others may expand their facilities, the number of new curator positions available will be extremely low, particularly compared to the number of interested job seekers. The number of curators employed by each facility depends upon the size and budget of the operation and the range of animal types they house.

STARTING OUT

The position of zoo and aquarium curator is seldom an entry-level job. Although there are exceptions, most curators start their careers as zookeepers or aquarists and move up through the animal management ranks.

Although the competition for zoo and aquarium jobs is intense, there are several ways to pursue such positions. Getting an education in animal science is a good way to make contacts that may be valuable in a job search. Professors and school administrators often can provide advice and counseling on finding jobs as a curator. The best sources for finding out about career opportunities at zoos and aquariums are trade journals (AZA's *Connect Magazine* or AAZK's *Animal Keepers' Forum),* the Web sites of specific institutions, and special-focus periodicals. Most zoos and aquariums have internal job postings. A few zoos and aquariums have job lines. People in the profession often learn about openings by word of mouth.

Working on a part-time or volunteer basis at an animal facility could provide an excellent opportunity to improve eligibility for higher level jobs in later years. Although many curators have worked in other positions in other fields before obtaining their jobs at animal facilities, others began their careers in lower level jobs at such places and worked their way up to where they wanted to be.

Moving up from a supervisory keeper position to a curatorial job usually involves moving out to another institution, often in another city and state.

ADVANCEMENT

Curatorial positions are often the top rung of the career ladder for many zoo and aquarium professionals. Curators do not necessarily wish to become zoo or aquarium directors, although the next step for specialized curators is to advance to the position of general curator. Those who are willing to forego direct involvement with animal management altogether and complete the transition to the business of running a zoo or aquarium will set as their ultimate goal the position of zoo or aquarium director. Curators who work for a small facility may aspire to a curatorial position at a larger zoo or aquarium, with greater responsibilities and a commensurate increase in pay.

Advancing to executive positions requires a combination of experience and education. General curators and zoo directors often have graduate degrees in zoology or in business or finance. Continuing professional education, such as AZA's courses in applied zoo and aquarium biology, conservation education, institutional record keeping, population management, and professional management, can be helpful. Attending workshops and conferences sponsored by professional groups or related organizations and making presentations is another means of networking with colleagues from other institutions and professions and becoming better known within the zoo world.

EARNINGS

Salaries of zoo and aquarium curators are widely varied, depending on the size and location of the institution, whether it is privately or publicly owned, the size of its endowments and budget, and on the curators' responsibilities, educational backgrounds, and experience. Generally, zoos and aquariums in metropolitan areas pay higher salaries.

The median annual salary for all curators was $47,930 in 2009, according to the U.S. Department of Labor. Salaries ranged from less than $27,000 to $83,900 or more.

Most zoos and aquariums provide benefits packages, including medical insurance, paid vacation and sick leave, and generous retirement benefits. As salaried employees, curators are not eligible for overtime pay, but they may get compensatory time for extra hours worked. Larger institutions may also offer coverage for prescription drugs, dental and vision insurance, mental health plans, and retirement savings plans. Private corporate zoos may offer better benefits, including profit sharing.

WORK ENVIRONMENT

The work atmosphere for curators of animal facilities will always center on the zoo or aquarium in which they work. Curators spend most of their time indoors at their desks, reading e-mail, talking on the phone, writing reports, meeting deadlines for budgets, planning exhibits, and so forth. Particularly at large institutions, the majority of their time is spent on administrative duties rather than hands-on interaction with animals. Like other zoo and aquarium employees, curators often work long hours tending to the varied duties to which they are assigned.

When the unexpected happens, curators get their share of animal emergencies. In difficult situations, they may find themselves working late into the night with keepers and veterinarians to help care for sick animals or those that are giving birth.

Curators are sometimes required to travel to conferences and community events. They might also travel to other zoos throughout the country or lead trips for zoo members to wilderness areas in the United States and abroad.

Despite the long hours, zoo and aquarium curators derive great personal satisfaction from their work.

OUTLOOK

There are only about 215 professionally operated zoos, aquariums, wildlife parks, and oceanariums in North America. Considering the number of people interested in animal careers, this is not a large number. Therefore, it is expected that competition for jobs as curators (as well as for most zoo and aquarium jobs) will continue to be very strong.

While employment opportunities for curators overall is projected to grow much faster than the average for all occupations through 2018, according to the U.S. Department of Labor, the outlook for zoo curators is not favorable. Because of the slow growth in new zoos and in their capacity to care for animals, job openings are not expected to grow rapidly. The prospects for aquarium curators is somewhat better due to planned construction of several new aquariums.

However, competition and low turnover rates will continue to squelch opportunities in these occupations. One area with greater growth potential than conventional zoos and aquariums is privately funded conservation centers.

FOR MORE INFORMATION

Visit the alliance's Web site for information on marine mammals, internships, and publications.

Alliance of Marine Mammal Parks and Aquariums
E-mail: ammpa@aol.com
http://www.ammpa.org

For information on membership, a list of accredited zoos throughout the world, and careers in aquatic and marine science, including job listings, contact

Association of Zoos and Aquariums
8403 Colesville Road, Suite 710
Silver Spring, MD 20910-3314
Tel: 301-562-0777
http://www.aza.org

Zoologists

OVERVIEW

Zoologists are biologists who study animals. They often select a particular type of animal to study, and they may study an entire animal, one part or aspect of an animal, or a whole animal society. There are many areas of specialization from which a zoologist can choose, such as origins, genetics, characteristics, classifications, behaviors, life processes, and distribution of animals.

HISTORY

The first important developments in zoology occurred in Greece, where Alcmaeon, a philosopher and physician, studied animals and performed the first known dissections of humans in the sixth century B.C. Aristotle, however, is generally considered to be the first real zoologist. Aristotle, who studied with the great philosopher Plato and tutored the world-conquering Alexander the Great, had the lofty goal of setting down in writing everything that was known in his time. In an attempt to extend that knowledge, he observed and dissected sea creatures. He also devised a system of classifying animals that included 500 species, a system that influenced scientists for many centuries after his death. Some scholars believe that Alexander sent various exotic animals to his old tutor from the lands he conquered, giving Aristotle unparalleled access to the animals of the ancient world.

With the exception of important work in physiology done by the Roman physician Galen, the study of zoology progressed little after Aristotle until the middle of the 16th century. Between 1555 and

QUICK FACTS

School Subjects
Biology
Chemistry
Earth science

Personal Skills
Communication/ideas
Technical/scientific

Work Environment
Indoors and outdoors
Primarily one location

Minimum Education Level
Bachelor's degree

Salary Range
$35,280 to $56,500 to $93,140+

Certification or Licensing
None available

Outlook
About as fast as the average

DOT
041

GOE
02.03.01, 02.03.03

NOC
2121

O*NET-SOC
19-1020.01, 19-1023.00

Largest Oceans in the World

Name	Square Miles	Greatest Depth
Pacific	60,060,700	36,198 feet
Atlantic	29,637,900	30,246 feet
Indian	26,469,500	24,460 feet
Southern	7,848,300	23,736 feet
Arctic	5,427,000	18,456 feet

Source: Information Please Database

1700, much significant work was done in the classification of species and in physiology, especially regarding the circulation of blood, which affected studies of both animals and humans. The invention of the microscope in approximately 1590 led to the discovery and study of cells. In the 18th century, Swedish botanist Carl Linnaeus developed the system of classification of plants and animals that is still used.

Zoology continued to develop at a rapid rate, and in 1859, Charles Darwin published *On the Origin of Species*, which promoted the theory of natural selection, revolutionized the way scientists viewed all living creatures, and gave rise to the field of ethology, the study of animal behavior. Since that time, innumerable advances have been made by zoologists throughout the world.

In the past century, the rapid development of technology has changed zoology and all sciences by giving scientists the tools to explore areas that had previously been closed to them. Computers, submersibles, high-definition cameras, Geographic Information Systems technology, satellites, and tremendously powerful microscopes are only a few of the means that modern zoologists have used to bring new knowledge to light. In spite of these advances, however, mysteries remain, questions go unanswered, and species wait to be discovered.

THE JOB

Although zoology is a single specialty within the field of biology, it is a vast specialty that includes many major subspecialties. Some zoologists study a single animal or a category of animals, whereas others may specialize in a particular part of an animal's anatomy or study a process that takes place in many kinds of animals. A zoologist might study single-cell organisms, a particular variety of fish, or the behavior of groups of animals such as whales or seals.

Many zoologists are classified according to the animals they study. For example, *entomologists* are experts on insects, *ichthyologists* study fish, *herpetologists* specialize in the study of reptiles and amphibians, *mammalogists* focus on mammals, and *ornithologists* study birds. *Embryologists,* however, are classified according to the process that they study. They examine the ways in which animal embryos form and develop from conception to birth.

Within each primary area of specialization there is a wide range of subspecialties. An ichthyologist, for example, might focus on the physiology, or physical structure and functioning, of a particular fish; on a biochemical phenomenon such as bioluminescence in deep-sea species; on the discovery and classification of fish; on variations within a single species in different parts of the world; or on the ways in which one type of fish interacts with other species in a specific environment. Others may specialize in the effects of pollution on fish or in finding ways to grow fish effectively in controlled environments in order to increase the supply of healthy food available for human consumption.

Some zoologists are primarily teachers, while others spend most of their time performing original research. Teaching jobs in universities and other facilities are probably the most secure positions available, but zoologists who wish to do extensive research may find such positions restrictive. Even zoologists whose primary function is research, however, often need to do some teaching in the course of their work, and almost everyone in the field has to deal with the public at one time or another.

Students often believe that zoological scientists spend most of their time in the field, observing animals and collecting specimens. In fact, most researchers spend no more than two to eight weeks in the field each year. Zoologists spend much of their time at a computer or on the telephone.

It is often the case that junior scientists spend more time in the field than do senior scientists, who study specimens and data collected in the field by their younger colleagues. Senior scientists spend much of their time coordinating research, directing younger scientists and technicians, and writing grant proposals or soliciting funds in other ways.

Raising money is an extremely important activity for zoologists who are not employed by government agencies or major universities. The process of obtaining money for research can be time consuming and difficult. Good development skills can also give scientists a flexibility that government-funded scientists do not have. Government money is sometimes available only for research in narrowly defined areas that may not be those that a scientist wishes to study. A zoologist who wants to study a particular area may seek his or her own funding in order not to be limited by government restrictions.

REQUIREMENTS

High School
To prepare for a career in zoology, make sure to get a well-rounded high school education. Although a solid grounding in biology and chemistry is an absolute necessity, you should remember that facility in English also will be invaluable. Writing monographs and articles, communicating with colleagues both orally and in writing, and writing persuasive fund-raising proposals are all activities at which scientists need to excel. You should also read widely, not merely relying on books on science or other subjects that are required by the school. The scientist-in-training should search the library for magazines and journals dealing with areas that are of personal interest. Developing the habit of reading will help prepare you for the massive amounts of reading involved in research and keeping up with latest developments in the field. Computer skills are also essential, since most zoologists not only use the computer for writing, communication, and research, but they also use various software programs to perform statistical analyses.

Postsecondary Training
A bachelor's degree is the minimum requirement to work as a zoologist; advanced degrees are needed for research or administrative work. Academic training, practical experience, and the ability to work effectively with others are the most important prerequisites for a career in zoology.

Other Requirements
Success in zoology requires tremendous effort. It would be unwise for a person who wants to work an eight-hour day to become a zoologist, since hard work and long hours (sometimes 60 to 80 hours per week) are the norm. Also, although some top scientists are paid extremely well, the field does not provide a rapid route to riches. A successful zoologist finds satisfaction in work, not in a paycheck. The personal rewards, however, can be tremendous. The typical zoologist finds his or her work satisfying on many levels.

A successful zoologist is generally patient and flexible. A person who cannot juggle various tasks will have a difficult time in a job that requires doing research, writing articles, dealing with the public, teaching students, soliciting funds, and keeping up with the latest publications in the field. Flexibility also comes into play when funding for a particular area of study ends or is unavailable. A zoologist whose range of expertise is too narrowly focused will be at a disad-

A zoologist sifts through fish bones taken from the spew of endangered Hawaiian monk seals at the Bishop Museum in Honolulu, Hawaii. The Hawaiian monk seal is one of the nation's most endangered marine mammals and the current research being done by zoologists is to determine the seal's diet by physically examining the remains of their meals. Numbering just 1,000, the Hawaiian monk seal has failed to rebound despite efforts to protect its main habitat in the Northwestern Hawaiian Islands. (*Marco Garcia, AP Photo*)

vantage when there are no opportunities in that particular area. A flexible approach and a willingness to explore various areas can be crucial in such situations, and a too-rigid attitude may lead a zoologist to avoid studies that he or she would have found rewarding.

An aptitude for reading and writing is a must for any zoologist. A person who hates to read would have difficulty keeping up with the literature in the field, and a person who cannot write or dislikes writing would be unable to write effective articles and books. Publishing is an important part of zoological work, especially for those who are conducting research.

EXPLORING

One of the best ways to find out if you are suited for a career as a zoologist is to talk to zoologists and find out exactly what they do. Contact experts in your field of interest. If you are interested in dolphins, find out whether there is a marine mammalogist in your area. If there is not, find an expert in some other part of the country. Read books, magazines, and journals to find out whom the experts are. Don't be afraid to write or call people and ask them questions.

One good way to meet experts is to attend meetings of professional organizations. If you are interested in fish, locate organizations of ichthyologists by searching in the library or on the Internet. If you can, attend an organization's meeting and introduce yourself to the attendees. Ask questions and learn as much as you can.

Try to become an intern or a volunteer at an organization that is involved in an area that you find interesting. Most organizations have internships, and if you look with determination for an internship, you are likely to find one.

EMPLOYERS

Zoologists are employed by a wide variety of institutions, not just zoos. Many zoologists are teachers at universities and other facilities, where they may teach during the year while spending their summers doing research. A large number of zoologists are researchers; they may be working for nonprofit organizations (requiring grants to fund their work), scientific institutions, or the government. Of course, there are many zoologists who are employed by zoos, aquariums, and museums. While jobs for zoologists exist all over the country, large cities that have universities, zoos, aquariums, and museums will provide far more opportunities for zoologists than in rural areas.

STARTING OUT

Though it is possible to find work with a bachelor's degree, it is likely that you will need to continue your education to advance further in the field. Competition for higher paying, high-level jobs among those with doctoral degrees is fierce; as a result, it is often easier to break into the field with a master's degree than it is with a Ph.D. Many zoologists with their master's degree seek a mid-level job and work toward a Ph.D. part time.

You will be ahead of the game if you have made contacts as an intern or as a member of a professional organization. It is an excellent idea to attend the meetings of professional organizations, which generally welcome students. At those meetings, introduce yourself to the scientists you admire and ask for their help and advice. Don't be shy, but be sure to treat people with respect. Ultimately, it is the way you relate to other people that determines how your career will develop.

ADVANCEMENT

Higher education and publishing are two of the most important means of advancing in the field of zoology. The holder of a Ph.D. will make more money and have a higher status than the holder of a bachelor's or master's degree. The publication of articles and books is important for both research scientists and professors of zoology. A young professor who does not publish cannot expect to become a full professor with tenure, and a research scientist who does not publish the results of his or her research will not become known as an authority in the field. In addition, the publication of a significant work lets everyone in the field know that the author has worked hard and accomplished something worthwhile.

Because zoology is not a career in which people typically move from job to job, people generally move up within an organization. A professor may become a full professor; a research scientist may become known as an expert in the field or may become the head of a department, division, or institution; a zoologist employed by an aquarium or a zoo may become an administrator or head curator. In some cases, however, scientists may not want what appears to be a more prestigious position. A zoologist who loves to conduct and coordinate research, for example, may not want to become an administrator who is responsible for budgeting, hiring and firing, and other tasks that have nothing to do with research.

EARNINGS

A 2009 survey conducted by the National Association of Colleges and Employers determined that holders of bachelor's degrees in biological and life sciences (including zoologists) earned average starting salaries of $33,254.

The median annual wage for zoologists in 2009 was $56,500, according to the U.S. Department of Labor. Salaries ranged from less than $35,280 to $93,140 or more. Zoologists who were employed by the federal government had mean annual earnings of $75,690.

It is possible for the best and brightest of zoologists to make substantial amounts of money. Occasionally, a newly graduated Ph.D. who has a top reputation may be offered a position that pays $100,000 or more per year, but only a few people begin their careers at such a high level.

The benefits that zoologists receive as part of their employment vary widely. Employees of the federal government or top universities tend to have extensive benefit packages, but the benefits offered by private industry cover a wide range, from extremely generous to almost nonexistent.

WORK ENVIRONMENT

There is much variation in the conditions under which zoologists work. Professors of zoology may teach exclusively during the school year or may both teach and conduct research. Many professors whose school year consists of teaching spend their summers doing research. Research scientists spend some time in the field, but most of their work is done in the laboratory. There are zoologists who spend most of their time in the field, but they are the exceptions to the rule.

Zoologists who do field work may have to deal with difficult conditions. For example, a shark expert may need to observe his subjects from a shark cage that has been lowered deep into the ocean. A marine ornithologist may have to walk the craggy shoreline during brisk weather to observe birds. For most people in the field, however, that aspect of the work is particularly interesting and satisfying.

Zoologists spend much of their time corresponding with others in their field, studying the latest literature, reviewing articles written by their peers, and making and returning phone calls. They also log many hours working with computers, using computer modeling, performing statistical analyses, recording the results of their research, or writing articles and grant proposals.

No zoologist works in a vacuum. Even those who spend much time in the field have to keep up with developments within their specialty. In most cases, zoologists deal with many different kinds of people, including students, mentors, the public, colleagues, representatives of granting agencies, private or corporate donors, reporters, and science writers. For this reason, the most successful members of the profession tend to develop good communication skills.

OUTLOOK

Employment for zoologists is expected to grow about as fast as the average for all careers through 2018, according to the U.S. Department of Labor. The field of zoology is relatively small, and competition for good positions—especially research positions—is high. High-level jobs are further limited by government budget cuts. Growth in the biological sciences should continue in the next decade, spurred partly by the need to analyze and offset the effects of pollution on the environment. Competition will be strongest for those with doctoral degrees. Those with a bachelor's or master's degree will face less competition due to a larger number of available positions—including those in nonscientist jobs related to zoology, such as marketing, sales, publishing, and research management. Those who are most successful in the field in the future are likely to be those who are able to diversify. Zoologists with expertise in a variety of animals or animal systems or processes will have strong employment prospects.

FOR MORE INFORMATION

Visit the alliance's Web site for information on marine mammals, internships, and publications.
Alliance of Marine Mammal Parks and Aquariums
E-mail: ammpa@aol.com
http://www.ammpa.org

The Education section of the institute's Web site has information on a number of careers in biology.
American Institute of Biological Sciences
1444 I Street, NW, Suite 200
Washington, DC 20005-6535
Tel: 202-628-1500
http://www.aibs.org

For information on membership, a list of accredited zoos through-out the world, and careers in aquatic and marine science, including job listings, contact

Association of Zoos and Aquariums
8403 Colesville Road, Suite 710
Silver Spring, MD 20910-3314
Tel: 301-562-0777
http://www.aza.org

The following society publishes the journal, Integrative and Comparative Biology, *and it is a good source of information about all areas and aspects of zoology. For more information, contact*

Society for Integrative and Comparative Biology
1313 Dolley Madison Boulevard, Suite 402
McLean, VA 22101-3926
Tel: 800-955-1236
E-mail: SICB@BurkInc.com
http://www.sicb.org

The association "promotes conservation, preservation, and propagation of animals in both private and public domains." It offers a membership category for those who support its goals.

Zoological Association of America
PO Box 511275
Punta Gorda, FL 33951-1275
Tel: 941-621-2021
E-mail: info@zaa.org
http://www.zaa.org

Index

Entries and page numbers in **bold** indicate major treatment of a topic.

A

AAZK. *See* American Association of Zoo Keepers, Inc. (AAZK)
Accreditation Board for Engineering and Technology (ABET) 147
acquisition editors 165
admiralty lawyers 119
Advancement section, explained 4
Agassiz, Alexander 22
Ahrens, Donald C. 17
Alcmaeon 185
Alexander the Great 185
Alliance of Marine Mammal Parks and Aquariums 138
American Academy of Underwater Sciences 63
American Association for the Advancement of Science (AAAS)
   Science & Technology Policy Fellowships 120–121, 123
American Association of University Professors 51–52
American Association of Wildlife Veterinarians 140
American Association of Zoo Keepers, Inc. (AAZK) 181–182
   Animal Keepers' Forum 182
American Association of Zoo Veterinarians 138, 140
American Bar Association 121, 123
American Board of Veterinary Specialties 138
American Boatbuilders and Repairers Association 129
American College of Veterinary Behaviorists 138
American College of Zoological Medicine 138
American Federation of Teachers 51–52
American Geophysical Union 105
American Meteorological Society 12, 15–18
American Society of Limnology and Oceanography
   biological oceanographers 27
   chemical oceanographers 38
   geological oceanographers 78, 79
   marine biologists 96, 97
   marine policy experts and lawyers 119
   physical oceanographers 157, 158
American Veterinary Medical Association (AVMA) 140
   American Board of Veterinary Specialties 138
   Council on Education 138
Anderson School of Natural History 43
animal curators 178
Animal Keepers' Forum 182
animal trainers. *See* marine mammal trainers

applied geophysicists 102
applied meteorologists 14
aquarists 5–11
   advancement 9–10
   aquariums (Web sites) 6
   certification or licensing 8
   earnings 10
   educational requirements 7–8
   employers 9
   employment outlook 10
   exploring the field 9
   high school requirements 7
   history 5, 7
   job, described 7
   for more information 11
   organizations 8, 9
   postsecondary training 8
   requirements 7–9
   starting out 9
   work environment 10
aquariums (Web sites) 6
Aristotle 12–13, 22, 43, 163, 185
Army Corps of Engineers 68
assistant curators 178
Association of American Veterinary Medical Colleges 140
Association of Zoos and Aquariums (AZA) 9, 179–182
   Connect Magazine 182
Atlantic Oceanographic and Meteorological Library
   Hurricane Research Division 18
The Atmosphere: An Introduction to Meteorology (Lutgens) 17
atmospheric chemists 36
atmospheric scientists 12–21
   advancement 18–19
   applied meteorologists 14
   certification or licensing 16–17
   climatologists 14
   dynamic meteorologists 14
   earnings 19
   earth systems science 14
   educational requirements 15–16
   employers 17–18
   employment outlook 20
   environmental meteorologists 14
   exploring the field 17
   flight meteorologists 14
   global research 14
   high school requirements 15
   history 12–13
   industrial meteorologists 14
   job, described 13–15
   for more information 20–21
   operational meteorologists 14
   organizations 12, 13, 15–18
   physical meteorologists 14
   postsecondary training 15–16
   requirements 15–17
   starting out 18
   synoptic meteorologists 14
   work environment 19–20

attorneys. *See* marine policy experts and
  lawyers
Audubon Aquarium of the Americas 5
AZA. *See* Association of Zoos and Aquariums (AZA)

B

Barnum, P. T. 177
bench repairers 128
biological oceanographers 1, 22–33
  advancement 27
  certification or licensing 25
  earnings 28
  educational requirements 25
  employers 26–27
  employment outlook 28–29
  exploring the field 26
  high school requirements 25
  history 22–23
  interview 31–33
  job, described 23–24
  for more information 29–31
  organizations 25, 26–27
  postsecondary training 25
  requirements 25–26
  starting out 27
  work environment 28
Biological Resources Discipline of the U.S.
  Geological Survey
  biological oceanographers 26–27
  chemical oceanographers 38
  generally 2
  geological oceanographers 79
  laboratory testing technicians 87
Bishop Museum 189
Bologna, University of 42
book editors 165
Boyle, Robert 163

C

Calvert Marine Museum 179
Cape Fear Community College 129
Challenger Reports 163
Chapman, Piers 54–58
chemical oceanographers 1, 34–41
  advancement 38
  atmospheric chemists 36
  certification or licensing 37
  earnings 38–39
  educational requirements 36–37
  employers 38
  employment outlook 39–40
  exploring the field 37–38
  high school requirements 36
  history 34–35
  job, described 35–36
  marine biochemists 36
  marine chemists 35
  marine geochemists 35–36
  for more information 40–41
  organizations 35, 38
  postsecondary training 36–37
  requirements 36–37
  starting out 38
  work environment 39
city editors 166

climatologists 14
coastal engineers. *See* ocean engineers
coastal geologists 76
**college professors, oceanography/marine sci-
  ence** 42–58
  advancement 49–50
  assistant professors 44
  associate professors 44
  correspondence instructors 46
  distance learning instructors 46
  earnings 50
  educational requirements 46–48
  employers 48–49
  employment outlook 51–52
  exploring the field 48
  extension work instructors 46
  full professors 44
  graduate assistants 45
  high school requirements 46
  history 42–43
  interview 54–58
  job, described 43–46
  junior college instructors 46
  for more information 52–54
  oceanography/marine science department
    chair 45
  online instructors 46
  organizations 51–52
  postsecondary training 46–48
  requirements 46–48
  starting out 49
  work environment 50–51
Connect Magazine 182
copy editors 166, 171
Cortes, Hernando 177

D

Darwin, Charles 22, 186
Dean John A. Knauss Marine Policy Fellowship 120, 123
decline, explained 4
Deep Sea Drilling Project (DSDP) 73
department editors 166
Department of Commerce. *See* U.S. Department of Commerce
Department of Defense. *See* U.S. Department
  of Defense
Department of Energy. *See* U.S. Department
  of Energy
Department of Labor. *See* U.S. Department
  of Labor
Department of the Interior. *See* U.S. Department of the Interior
The Depths of the Sea (Thompson) 163
development engineers 146
Dictionary of Occupational Titles (DOT) 3
did you know?
  science writers and editors 167
Distributions of Marine Life (Forbes) 163
divers and diving technicians 59–72
  advancement 68–69
  certification or licensing 66
  diving safety officers 63
  earnings 69–70
  educational requirements 65–66

employers 67–68
employment outlook 71
exploring the field 67
high school requirements 65
history 59–60, 62
job, described 62–64
for more information 71–72
organizations 66
postsecondary training 65–66
recreation specialists 59
requirements 65–67
starting out 68
tenders 69
Web sites 61
work environment 70–71
diving safety officers 63
doctors of veterinary medicine. *See* marine
veterinarians
DolphinTrainer.com 112
dynamic meteorologists 14

E

Earnings section, explained 4
earth systems science 14
ECOHAB (Ecology and Oceanography of
Harmful Algal Blooms) 155
editor in chief 171
editors. *See* science writers and editors
eGFI: Dream Up the Future: Ocean Engineering 148
embryologists 187
Employers section, explained 4
Employment Outlook section, explained 4
*Encyclopedia of Careers and Vocational
Guidance* (Ferguson) 3
engineers. *See* ocean engineers
entomologists 187
environmental meteorologists 14
Environmental Protection Agency
biological oceanographers 26
chemical oceanographers 35, 38
geological oceanographers 79
laboratory testing technicians 87
exploration geophysicists 102
Exploring section, explained 3–4

F

fact checkers 166
Federal Communications Commission 129
fiberglass repairers 128
field repairers 128
first assistant editors 171
flight meteorologists 14
Forbes, Edward 163
For More Information section, explained 4
4-H 139

G

Galen 185
Garrison, Tom S. 78
geochronologists 76
geological oceanographers 1, 73–84
advancement 79
certification or licensing 78
coastal geologists 76

earnings 79
educational requirements 77–78
employers 78–79
employment outlook 80
exploring the field 78
geochronologists 76
high school requirements 77
history 73–74
job, described 74–77
for more information 80–84
organizations 78, 79
paleontologists 76
petrologists 76
postsecondary training 77–78
requirements 77–78
seismologists 76
starting out 79
words to learn 75
work environment 80
Geological Society of America 79, 105
geophysical prospectors 102
geophysicists. *See* marine geophysicists
Georges Bank fishery 118
Georgia Aquarium 5
growth, explained 4
Guide for Occupational Exploration
(GOE) 3

H

Hallock-Muller, Pamela 31–33
herpetologists 187
Histoire Physique de la Mer (Marsigli) 163
Historia Animalium (Aristotle) 22, 43, 163
History section, explained 3
HMS *Challenger* 34, 91, 153–154, 163
HMS *Lightning* 91
HMS *Porcupine* 91
Human Resources and Skills Development
Canada 3
Hurricane Research Division 18
hydrologists 102

I

ichthyologists 187
Imperial Menagerie of the Schönbrunn Zoo
177
industrial meteorologists 14
Integrated Ocean Drilling Program (IODP)
74, 76
International Association of Aquatic Animal
Medicine 138
International Council for the Exploration of
the Sea 23
International Marine Animal Trainers' Asso-
ciation 109
International Meteorological Association 13
International Meteorological Congress 13
International Program of Ocean Drilling
(IPOD) 73–74
interviews
biological oceanographers 31–33
college professors, oceanography/marine
science 54–58
Invitation to Oceanography (Pinet) 23, 34,
154

J

JIST Works 3
Job section, explained 3
John G. Shedd Aquarium 5
Junior Engineering Technological Society
   (JETS) 148

L

laboratory testing technicians 85–90
   advancement 88
   earnings 88
   educational requirements 86
   employers 87–88
   employment outlook 89
   exploring the field 87
   high school requirements 86
   history 85
   job, described 85–86
   for more information 89–90
   organizations 87
   postsecondary training 86
   requirements 86–87
   starting out 88
   work environment 88–89
largest oceans in the world 186
lawyers. *See* marine policy experts and lawyers
*Life at the Zoo: Behind the Scenes with the
   Animal Doctors* (Robinson) 139
Limnology and Oceanography 45
line editors 166
Linnaeus, Carl 186
London Zoological Society 177
Lutgens, Frederick K. 17

M

magazine editors 166
managing editors 171
marine biochemists 36
Marine Biological Laboratory 23, 43
marine biologists 23, 91–100
   advancement 96–97
   aquatic chemical ecology 95
   bioinformatics 95
   books to read 92
   certification or licensing 95
   earnings 97
   educational requirements 94–95
   employers 96
   employment outlook 98
   exploring the field 95
   high school requirements 94
   history 91–92
   job, described 92–94
   marine biotechnologists 94
   for more information 98–100
   organizations 95–97
   postsecondary training 94–95
   requirements 94–95
   starting out 96
   work environment 97–98
marine biotechnologists 94
marine chemists 35
marine electronics technicians 128
marine geochemists 35–36
marine geophysicists 101–108

advancement 105
applied geophysicists 102
earnings 105–106
educational requirements 103–104
employers 104
employment outlook 106
exploration geophysicists 102
exploring the field 104
geophysical prospectors 102
high school requirements 103
history 101
hydrologists 102
job, described 102–103
for more information 106–108
organizations 104, 105
party chiefs 105
postsecondary training 103–104
requirements 103–104
seismologists 102–103
starting out 104–105
tectonophysicists 103
volcanologists 103
work environment 106
marine mammal trainers 109–116
   advancement 114
   certification or licensing 112
   earnings 114
   educational requirements 110–112
   employers 113
   employment outlook 115
   exploring the field 112–113
   high school requirements 110–111
   history 109
   job, described 110
   for more information 115–116
   organizations 109, 112
   postsecondary training 111–112
   requirements 110–112
   starting out 113–114
   work environment 114–115
marine policy experts and lawyers
   117–126
   admiralty lawyers 119
   advancement 124
   certification or licensing 121
   earnings 124
   educational requirements 120–121
   employers 123
   employment outlook 125
   exploring the field 122–123
   high school requirements 120
   history 117–118
   job, described 118–119
   maritime lawyers, generally 119
   maritime policy lawyers 119
   for more information 125–126
   organizations 119–121, 123
   postsecondary training 120–121
   requirements 120–122
   starting out 123–124
   work environment 124–125
marine services technicians 127–134
   advancement 132
   bench repairers 128
   certification or licensing 129–130
   earnings 132
   educational requirements 129

employers 131
employment outlook 133
exploring the field 130–131
fiberglass repairers 128
field repairers 128
high school requirements 129
history 127
job, described 127–128
marine electronics technicians
  128
marine surveyors 132
for more information 133–134
motorboat mechanics 128
organizations 129–131
postsecondary training 129
requirements 129–130
starting out 131
work environment 132–133
marine surveyors 132
Marine Technology Society
  biological oceanographers 27
  chemical oceanographers 38
  geological oceanographers 79
  ocean engineers 148
  physical oceanographers 158
Marine Trades Association of New Jersey
  131
marine veterinarians 135–143
  advancement 140–141
  certification or licensing 138–139
  earnings 141
  educational requirements 137–138
  employers 140
  employment outlook 141
  exploring the field 139
  high school requirements 137
  history 135
  job, described 136–137
  for more information 141–143
  organizations 138–140
  postsecondary training 137–138
  requirements 137–140
  starting out 140
  work environment 141
maritime policy lawyers 119
Marsigli, Luigi 163
Mashima, Ted Y. 139
Maury, Matthew Fontaine 153, 163
Mayfield, Max 16
Merchant Marine Corps 68
Meteor 23, 34, 154
Meteorologica (Aristotle) 13
meteorologists. *See* atmospheric scientists
*Meteorology Today: An Introduction to
  Weather, Climate, and the Environment*
  (Ahrens) 17
Miami Seaquarium 7, 177
Miami, University of
  Rosenstiel School of Marine and Atmo-
    spheric Science 26, 37
Michigan Boating Industries Association
  131
Mid-Atlantic Marine Education Associa-
  tion 96
Minerals Management Service
  biological oceanographers 26

geological oceanographers 79
laboratory testing technicians 87
Monterey Bay Aquarium 7
Moorpark College 111
motorboat mechanics 128
Murray, John 22, 34, 91
The Museum of America and the Sea 129

N

National Aeronautics and Space Administra-
  tion
  atmospheric scientists 18
  biological oceanographers 26
  generally 2
  geological oceanographers 79
  laboratory testing technicians 87
National Aquarium (Baltimore) 5
National Association of Colleges and
  Employers 97, 149
National Center for Atmospheric Research
  18
National Geodetic Survey 105
National Geological Survey 105
National Hurricane Center 16
National Marine Electronics Association
  130
National Marine Fisheries Service 96
National Occupational Classification (NOC)
  Index 3
National Oceanic and Atmospheric Administration (NOAA)
  atmospheric scientists 13, 17, 18
  biological oceanographers 26
  generally 2
  geological oceanographers 79
  laboratory testing technicians 87
  marine biologists 96
  National Marine Fisheries Service 96
  ocean engineers 144
National Park Service 26, 79
National Science Foundation
  atmospheric scientists 18
  biological oceanographers 26
  generally 2
  geological oceanographers 73, 74,
    78–79
  laboratory testing technicians 87
  marine policy experts and lawyers 119
National Sea Grant (NSG) College Program
  Dean John A. Knauss Marine Policy Fel-
    lowship 120
National Weather Association 17
National Weather Service 17, 18, 20
NAUI Worldwide 66
naval and marine engineers 145
naval architects 145
Naval Oceanographic Office
  generally 2
  geological oceanographers 79
  laboratory testing technicians 87
  marine geophysicists 105
Naval Research Laboratory 26, 79
NCEFS 147
newspaper editors 166
New York Aquarium 5

New York Times 168
NOAA. *See* National Oceanic and Atmospheric Administration (NOAA)

O

Observations and Experiments on the Saltiness of the Sea (Boyle) 163
Occupational Information Network (O*NET)-Standard Occupational Classification System (SOC) Index 3
Occupational Outlook Handbook
   atmospheric scientists 20
   generally 4
   marine geophysicists 106
Ocean Drilling Program 74
ocean engineers 144–152
   advancement 149
   certification or licensing 147
   coastal engineers, generally 145
   development engineers 146
   earnings 149
   educational requirements 146–147
   employers 148
   employment outlook 150
   exploring the field 148
   high school requirements 146–147
   history 144
   job, described 144–146
   for more information 150––152
   naval and marine engineers 145
   naval architects 145
   organizations 144, 147
   postsecondary training 147
   project engineers 146
   quick facts 145
   requirements 146–148
   starting out 148–149
   work environment 149–150
oceanographers. *See* biological oceanographers; chemical oceanographers; geological oceanographers; physical oceanographers
oceanographic engineers. *See* ocean engineers
Oceanographic Institute (Monaco) 177
Oceanography 45
oceanography and marine science Web sites 61
Oceanography: An Invitation to Marine Science (Garrison) 78
The Oceanography Society
   biological oceanographers 27
   chemical oceanographers 38
   generally 2
   geological oceanographers 79
   laboratory testing technicians 87
   physical oceanographers 157
Office of Naval Research
   biological oceanographers 27
   generally 2
   geological oceanographers 79
   laboratory testing technicians 87
Office of Naval Research Marine Meteorology Program 18
On the Origin of Species (Darwin) 186
operational meteorologists 14

ornithologists 187
Outlook section, explained 4
Overview section, explained 3
Oxford University 42–43

P

PADI
   biological oceanographers 8
   divers and diving technicians 66
   geological oceanographers 78
   marine biologists 95
   marine mammal trainers 112
Padre Island National Seashore (Texas) 93
paleontologists 76
Paris, University of 42
party chiefs 105
petrologists 76
The Physical Geography of the Sea (Maury) 153, 163
physical meteorologists 14
physical oceanographers 1–2, 153–161
   advancement 158
   books to read 154
   certification or licensing 157
   earnings 158–159
   educational requirements 155–157
   employers 158
   employment outlook 159
   exploring the field 157
   high school requirements 155–156
   history 153–154
   job, described 154–155
   for more information 160–161
   organizations 155, 157, 158
   postsecondary training 156–157
   requirements 155–157
   starting out 158
   work environment 159
Pinet, Paul R. 23, 34, 154
Plato 185
PopSci.com 1
PPG Aquarium 8
production editors 165
project engineers 146
Project Mohole 73
proofreaders 166
public information officers 162
Publishers Weekly 170

Q

Quick Facts section, explained 3

R

recreation specialists 59
Regents Park (London) 5, 177
Requirements section, explained 3
The Rhino with Glue-On Shoes: And Other Surprising Trues Stories of Zoo Vets and Their Patients (Spelman and Mashima) 139
Robinson, Phillip T. 139
Rosenstiel School of Marine and Atmospheric Science 26, 37
Ross, James 22
Ross, John 22

S

Samansky, Terry S. 112
Santa Margarita 60
Schönbrunn Zoo 177
science writers and editors 162–175
    acquisition editors 165
    advancement 170–171
    book editors 165
    city editors 166
    copy editors 166, 171
    department editors 166
    did you know? 167
    earnings 171–172
    editor in chief 171
    educational requirements 166–168
    employers 169
    employment outlook 173
    exploring the field 168–169
    fact checkers 166
    first assistant editors 171
    high school requirements 166
    history 162–164
    job, described 164–166
    line editors 166
    magazine editors 166
    managing editors 171
    for more information 173–175
    newspaper editors 166
    organizations 169
    postsecondary training 166–168
    production editors 165
    proofreaders 166
    public information officers 162
    requirements 166–168
    senior copy editors 171
    staff writers 166
    starting out 169–170
    work environment 172–173
Scripps Institution of Oceanography
    aquarists 5
    biological oceanographers 23, 24, 26
    chemical oceanographers 37
    college professors, oceanography/marine
        science 43, 49
    marine biologists 96
    zoo and aquarium curators 177
Sea Grant College and Programs Act (1966)
    43
Sea Grant Marine Careers Web site
    chemical oceanographers 37
    divers and diving technicians 67
    geological oceanographers 76, 78
    marine biologists 95
    marine geophysicists 104
    marine policy experts and lawyers 122
    marine services technicians 131
    ocean engineers 148
    physical oceanographers 155, 157
Sea World 177
Seismological Society of America 105
seismologists 76, 102–103
senior copy editors 171
Shedd Aquarium 110
Smithsonian Institution
    Division of Fishes, National Museum of
        Natural History 5
Society for Technical Communications 169

South Florida, University of 31–33
Spelman, Lucy H. 139
staff writers 166
Starting Out section, explained 4
*Starting Your Career as a Marine Mammal
    Trainer* (Samansky) 112
Steinhart Aquarium 5
Stellwagen Bank 74
Student Lawyer 123
synoptic meteorologists 14

T

tectonophysicists 103
tenders 69
Texas A&M University 54–58
Thomson, Charles Wyville 22, 34, 91, 163
Titanic 62
Torricelli, Evangelista 13

U

U.S. Bureau of Labor Statistics 4
U.S. Department of Agriculture 18, 140
U.S. Department of Commerce
    biological oceanographers 26
    generally 2
    geological oceanographers 79
    laboratory testing technicians 87
U.S. Department of Defense
    atmospheric scientists 18
    biological oceanographers 26
    generally 2
    geological oceanographers 79
    laboratory testing technicians 87
U.S. Department of Energy
    biological oceanographers 26
    generally 2
    geological oceanographers 79
    laboratory testing technicians 87
U.S. Department of Homeland Security 140
U.S. Department of Labor
    aquarists 10
    atmospheric scientists 19
    biological oceanographers 28
    chemical oceanographers 38–39
    college professors, oceanography/marine
        science 50–51
    divers and diving technicians 69, 71
    generally 2, 3
    geological oceanographers 79, 80
    laboratory testing technicians 88
    marine biologists 97
    marine geophysicists 105
    marine mammal trainers 114, 115
    marine policy experts and lawyers 124
    marine services technicians 132
    marine veterinarians 141
    ocean engineers 149, 150
    physical oceanographers 159
    science writers and editors 171–173
    zoo and aquarium curators 183–184
    zoologists 192–193
U.S. Department of the Interior
    biological oceanographers 26
    generally 2
    geological oceanographers 79
    laboratory testing technicians 87

U.S. Fish Commission 43
U.S. Geological Survey
    Biological Resources Discipline 26–27,
    38, 79, 87
U.S. National Science Foundation. *See*
    National Science Foundation
U.S. Navy 60, 68
USS *Albatross* 23

V
veterinarians. *See* marine veterinarians
Virginia, University of 43
volcanologists 103

W
Washington, University of
    School of Oceanography 96
Washington County Community College
    129
Wen Wang 177
WoodenBoat School 129
Woods Hole Oceanographic Institute
    aquarists 5
    biological oceanographers 23, 24, 26
    chemical oceanographers 37
    college professors, oceanography/marine
        science 43, 49
    geological oceanographers 78
Work Environment section, explained 4
World Meteorological Organization (WMO)
    13

Y
YMCA 66

Z
zoo and aquarium curators 176–184
    advancement 182–183
    animal curators 178

assistant curators 178
    earnings 183
    educational requirements 180
    employers 181
    employment outlook 184
    exploring the field 181
    high school requirements 180
    history 176–177
    job, described 177–180
    for more information 184
    organizations 177, 179–182
    postsecondary training 180
    requirements 180–181
    starting out 182
    work environment 183–184
zoologists 185–194
    advancement 191
    earnings 192
    educational requirements 188
    embryologists 187
    employers 190
    employment outlook 193
    entomologists 187
    exploring the field 190
    herpetologists 187
    high school requirements 188
    history 185–186
    ichthyologists 187
    job, described 186–188
    largest oceans in the world 186
    for more information 193–194
    ornithologists 187
    postsecondary training 188
    requirements 188–190
    starting out 191
    work environment 192–193